Melk
the Christmas Monkey

Teaching God's Character through Bible
Lessons and Activities the Entire Family
Can Enjoy

Melk, the Christmas Monkey
by Katie Hornor
Artwork by Kat Reader

Published by *Lemonhass*®

Printed in the USA by Create Space
ISBN-13: 978-1500945701
ISBN-10: 1500945706

Scripture quotations are from the King James Version Scripture quotations are from the King James Version (The Holy Bible, King James Version) Public Domain. Definitions from *Noah Webster's 1828 American Dictionary of the English Language*. 2014. http:// 1828.mshaffer.com (1 September 2014).

About the Author

Katie and her husband Tap have been missionaries in Mexico since 2007. They homeschool their five children, and in addition to their local ministry have an online bookstore and have developed a homeschool curriculum in the Spanish language.

Katie is an international speaker, educator, author and blogger who loves Christmas inside and out. She often starts counting down the days until Christmas as soon as the Fourth of July is over, and breaks out the Christmas music mid-October! *Melk, the Christmas Monkey* came

about as the Hornors sought a way to establish meaningful family traditions while creating fun and fond memories with their children during the Christmas season.

Two of Katie's many favorite sayings are: "Life's too short to be ordinary." and "Some people seek happiness; others create it." And she keeps creating. Besides *Melk, the Christmas Monkey*, she has authored over 40 titles, including the *Lemonhass*® Pre-K - Sixth grade homeschool curriculum for Spanish Speaking families.

Katie blogs about intentional praise in marriage, motherhood, homeschooling and ministry at ParadisePraises.com and coaches midlife women bloggers to make more and impact more at BloggingSuccessfully.com and TheBlogConnection.com

See also:
https://paradisepraises.com/about
http://tkhornor.com/
https://katiehornor.com/about

Contents

Introduction for Parents
Introduction for the Children (to be read/shared with your children when *Melk* is introduced).

January - November monthly lessons for optional monthly support.

Introduction for Parents

Melk, The Christmas Monkey, is a way of teaching God's character to children through 30 fun, Bible lessons and activities for the entire family to enjoy during the Christmas season. These ideas could also be easily adapted for a Sunday school class or children's Bible club.

While at our house *Melk* is a Christmas Monkey, at your house he could actually be a monkey, moose, mallard, MaCaw, mongoose, mouse, manatee, mackerel, magpie, mantis, meerkat, mole, mockingbird, mountain goat, etc... you are free to choose your animal (or doll) and give him/her your own name if you like. It doesn't have to be *Melk*, just make it meaningful. If you already have a Christmas friend who helps you count down the days until Christmas, you can easily adapt these lessons to fit that character. If you don't have a Christmas friend, please visit https://paradisepraises.com/melk-monkey for suggestions and links to where to purchase one.

Each of the 30 lessons and activities will give a good explanation of the character trait and conversation points as you go throughout your day. Feel free to choose the activities that your family most needs or would most enjoy, though you may choose to do them all! You can start December first, earlier or later, as you wish, or just do one every other day and make the fun stretch for two seasons. It's all up to you!

The lessons are organized in a suggested order. However, feel free to rearrange the order to fit your family's schedule, activities and resources. For instance, if your family has a December birthday, trade that day with day 9 on the list. And if your family doesn't have a December birthday, you might skip that activity or save it for the 25th to celebrate Jesus' birthday. If you know you have a Christmas concert coming up on a certain day, or are taking a trip for the holidays, assign that activity to that day on your schedule. The only one that I highly suggest to do towards the beginning is #2, the *Advent (Countdown) Paper Chain activity, as it will help you count down each day in anticipation of Christmas Day. If you need help with planning out your activities, please visit www.MelkLinks.com for a free printable calendar you can use to schedule *Melk's* activities along with your family's December schedule.

Our family usually introduces *Melk* on November 30. Sometimes he even gets to be "discovered" wrapped as a gift: the "first gift of Christmas" to kick off the Christmas season in our home. Throughout the season *Melk* is "discovered" again and again in some pretty crazy positions and situations, so the more flexible and easy to pose he is, the better!

Each night you will need to secretly set the scene with *Melk* and his props for your children to find in the morning. You may wish to download his letters and print them out to place with him each night, or you may read his letters right from your book. Some of the lessons also include a link to a resource or printable activity that you can do together. Some of the activities are more parent work-intensive than others and you may need to purchase a few things ahead of time if you don't have them at home already.

All of the props, materials and links to instructions and printables are clearly marked on each activity description, but take into account what you have on hand and what you may need to get and/or print as you plan your activities. Melk's letters, journal pages, printables, and other Christmas resources may be found at www.MelkLinks.com.

Melk's printable letters have a number on them corresponding to the number in the Table of Contents. You may download the letters from *Melk* to your kids that are print ready. Or you may download the same set of letters, but without the greeting or *Melk's* signature on them, so that you can write in your child's name to make it more personal, and/or sign it from your own special friend if he has a different name. You will also find a final good-bye letter in the downloads, if you choose to use it.

We would love to have you to share photos of your family and *Melk* on social media. You can follow our Facebook page and tag us (https://www.facebook.com/paradisepraises) or share on your social media using the hashtag #Melk or #MelktheChristmasMonkey, and be sure to tell us what state or country you represent. Our family's goal is to see *Melk* teaching God's character to families all over the world!

Melk's Facebook Fan Club: https://www.facebook.com/groups/MelksFanClub/
Melk's Instagram Account: https://instagram.com/MelkTheChristmasMonkey

Introduction for the Children

To be read/shared with your children when *Melk* is introduced.

This is *Melk*, the Christmas Monkey (read "friend" if using a different friend).

Melk's real name is Melchior Noël Yule. But he likes to be called *Melk* for short. This is what his long name means:

Melchior = the supposed name of one of the wise men who visited Jesus as a child and brought him gifts (That event is what some people call the first Christmas).

Noël = a french word for birthday, is also another word for Christmas in some countries.

Yule = of Christmas time, it is one of the oldest names for the Christmas season and celebration.

Melk loves Christmas because this is the time of year when more people than usual think about God and his free gift of salvation. If there is anything *Melk* loves more than Christmas it is God. *Melk* loves to learn about God and to share what he learns with others.

This year *Melk* has chosen our family for a special adventure. He plans to spend the month of December with us teaching us something about God's character each day until Christmas. Studying God's character, we get to know him, and getting to know him makes us wise.

There are three other important things you should know about *Melk*, however:
1. *Melk* is a *nocturnal* monkey. That means that he likes to sleep during the day and usually is only active very late at night.
2. He is also a *mute* monkey. That means he can't talk. Everything he will teach you will be by writing letters. Similar to how God wrote us letters in the Bible. All of his other senses work fine though. He can see and hear and he feels touch very well, which leads me to the next thing…

3. *Melk* doesn't like to be touched. He is a VERY sensitive monkey, so it might be good to find a special spot in your house where he can be comfortable each day and still see and hear all the fun you're having with his activities, and catch up on his rest. And remember, if anyone touches him or needs to move him, it should be Mom or Dad, (because they know how to be super gentle).

So find a spot for *Melk*, and say good night. Then be sure to look for him and his first letter bright and early in the morning!

MELK'S PHOTO GALLERY

Only 1 more day till Christmas!

¡Feliz Navidad!

PLEASE VISIT

WWW.FACEBOOK.COM/PARADISEPRAISES

TO SHARE YOUR PICTURES OF **MELK** WITH US. BE SURE TO TELL US WHERE YOU LIVE. WE WOULD LOVE TO HAVE EVERY COUNTRY AND CONTINENT OF THE WORLD REPRESENTED!

PAPER PLATE ANGEL

MELK:

IS FOUND DRAWING A PICTURE OF AN ANGEL

ACTIVITY:

MAKE PAPER PLATE ANGELS (DOWNLOAD TEMPLATE AND INSTRUCTIONS AT WWW.MELKLINKS.COM

MATERIALS:

PAPER PLATE, PENCIL, SCISSORS (OPTIONAL: HOLE PUNCHES)

LESSON:

GOD SENDS HIS ANGELS TO TAKE CARE OF US.

SCRIPTURE:

FOR HE SHALL GIVE HIS ANGELS CHARGE OVER THEE, TO KEEP THEE IN ALL THY WAYS. PSALM 91:11

Care

n. Charge or oversight, implying concern for safety and prosperity; as, he was under the care of a physician.

Good morning!

Today I'd like to teach you about God's care for us. Did you know that God has angels on duty all the time just to watch over us?

Psalm 91:11 says: For he shall give his angels charge over thee, to keep thee in all thy ways.

You and I must be pretty important for God to take care of us like that! Let's thank him for being a loving and caring God.

You can see I've been busy drawing an angel for you. Today as you make a paper plate angel I want you to talk about all the ways that God takes care of you and protects you.

Your Friend, Melk

GOD KEEPS HIS PROMISES

Promise

n. a declaration, written or verbal, made by one person to another, which binds the person who makes it, either in honor, conscience or law, to do or forbear a certain act specified.

ADVENT (COUNTDOWN) CHAIN

NOTE: YOU MAY WANT TO DO THIS ACTIVITY EARLY ON, SO YOU CAN USE IT TO COUNT DOWN THE DAYS UNTIL CHRISTMAS.

MELK:

IS FOUND WITH ADVENT CALENDAR OR COUNTDOWN PAPER CHAIN MATERIALS, MAYBE HAVING MADE A TINY ONE HIMSELF

ACTIVITY:

INTRODUCE THE ADVENT CALENDAR AND OR MAKE COUNTDOWN PAPER CHAIN. EVERYDAY AFTER, YOU MAY TAKE OFF ONE LINK OF THE CHAIN UNTIL YOU GET TO CHRISTMAS.

MATERIALS:

YOUR OWN ADVENT CALENDAR OR SCISSORS, TAPE (OR STAPLER), STRIPS OF COLORED PAPER (ENOUGH TO COUNT ONE FOR EVERY DAY UNTIL CHRISTMAS.)

LESSON:

SCRIPTURE TELLS US TO WATCH AND WAIT, WE COUNT DOWN THE DAYS TILL WE CELEBRATE CHRIST'S BIRTH, BUT WE DON'T KNOW WHEN HE WILL COME BACK. WE KNOW HE WILL THOUGH BECAUSE HE KEEPS HIS PROMISES.

SCRIPTURE:

KNOW THEREFORE THAT THE LORD THY GOD, HE IS GOD, THE FAITHFUL GOD, WHICH KEEPETH COVENANT AND MERCY WITH THEM THAT LOVE HIM AND KEEP HIS COMMANDMENTS TO A THOUSAND GENERATIONS. DEUTERONOMY 7:9

BLESSED BE THE LORD, THAT HATH GIVEN REST UNTO HIS PEOPLE ISRAEL, ACCORDING TO ALL THAT HE PROMISED: THERE HATH NOT FAILED ONE WORD OF ALL HIS GOOD PROMISE, WHICH HE PROMISED BY THE HAND OF MOSES HIS SERVANT. 1 KINGS 8:56

BE YE ALSO PATIENT; STABLISH YOUR HEARTS: FOR THE COMING OF THE LORD DRAWETH NIGH. JAMES 5:8

Hi Guys!

I am counting down the days 'til Christmas because I LOVE Christmas! Counting down to Christmas is also called "advent" which means the waiting time. For many many years God promised the world that his Son, the Messiah would come, and when Jesus was born in Bethlehem, it was God keeping his promise. "There hath not failed one word of all his good promise, which he promised by the hand of Moses his servant" (1 Kings 8:56).

 (continued on next page)

There is another promise God has made to us. That he will come back to earth to get all of his children some day. "Be ye also patient; stablish your hearts: for the coming of the Lord draweth nigh" (James 5:8). Just like he has kept his promises throughout history, we know he will keep that promise too and we can wait for his coming. In the meantime though, lets make a paper chain today for Advent, to count down the waiting days until Christmas!

Excitedly, Melk

GOD LOVES GOOD MEMORIES

Memory

n. A retaining of past ideas in the mind; remembrance.

TAKE FAMILY PHOTOS

NOTE: YOU MAY WANT THIS TO BE ONE OF YOUR FIRST ACTIVITIES, SO THAT YOU CAN INCLUDE MELK IN YOUR PHOTO AND GET THEM PRINTED IN TIME TO INCLUDE WITH YOUR CHRISTMAS GREETING CARDS.

MELK:

IS FOUND LOOKING AT LAST YEAR'S CHRISTMAS PHOTOS AND CHRISTMAS CARDS OR LINING UP SOME TOY FRIENDS AND TAKING THEIR PHOTO

ACTIVITY:

TAKE THIS YEAR'S FAMILY CHRISTMAS PICTURE. IF YOU NEED SOME IDEAS, CHECK OUT OUR CHRISTMAS PHOTO IDEAS LINK AT

WWW.MELKLINKS.COM

MATERIALS:

LAST YEAR'S CHRISTMAS PICTURES, CAMERA AND SMILES

LESSON:

GOD WANTS US TO HAVE THINGS THAT CAUSE US TO REMEMBER AND TELL OTHERS ABOUT WHAT HE HAS DONE FOR US.

SCRIPTURE:

AND HE SPAKE UNTO THE CHILDREN OF ISRAEL, SAYING, WHEN YOUR CHILDREN SHALL ASK THEIR FATHERS IN TIME TO COME, SAYING, WHAT MEAN THESE STONES? THEN YE SHALL LET YOUR CHILDREN KNOW, SAYING, ISRAEL CAME OVER THIS JORDAN ON DRY LAND. FOR THE LORD YOUR GOD DRIED UP THE WATERS OF JORDAN FROM BEFORE YOU, UNTIL YE WERE PASSED OVER, AS THE LORD YOUR GOD DID TO THE RED SEA, WHICH HE DRIED UP FROM BEFORE US, UNTIL WE WERE GONE OVER: THAT ALL THE PEOPLE OF THE EARTH MIGHT KNOW THE HAND OF THE LORD, THAT IT IS MIGHTY: THAT YE MIGHT FEAR THE LORD YOUR GOD FOR EVER. JOSHUA 4:21-24

Hello!

Don't you love pictures! I just love taking them and then looking at them and remembering all the fun times we've had, and all the wonderful things God has done for us.

    (continued on next page)

Do you remember the story of the Israelites crossing the Jordan River on dry land after their years in the desert (Joshua 4)? After they were safe on the other side and had thanked and praised God, God told them to set up a memorial of stones. That way whenever their children saw it and asked what it was for, they could tell the story of the goodness and miracle of God in saving them! What a great memory!

Today I want you to look through your Christmas pictures from last year and remember what God has done. And then you're going to take some family photos, so that in the future we can remember how good God has been to you this year too, and in this Christmas season. Remember the good things!

Your Remembering Friend, Melk

GOD'S WORD IS SWEET

Sweet

a. Agreeable or grateful to the taste; as, sugar or honey is sweet.

CANDY TREATS

MELK:

IS FOUND GETTING STUCK WHILE TRYING TO GET INTO A BAG, OR JAR, OF CANDY (KISSES, M&MS, CHOCOLATE CHIPS, ETC)

ACTIVITY:

ENJOY A SWEET TREAT TOGETHER

MATERIALS:

CANDY, JAR OR BAG

LESSON:

GOD IS GOOD, AND HIS WORD IS GOOD. GOD'S WORD IS TO THE SOUL LIKE SWEET FOOD TO THE BODY. A JOY TO SAVOR!

SCRIPTURE:

O TASTE AND SEE THAT THE LORD IS GOOD: BLESSED IS THE MAN THAT TRUSTETH IN HIM. PSALM 34:8

THE LAW OF THE LORD IS PERFECT, CONVERTING THE SOUL: THE TESTIMONY OF THE LORD IS SURE, MAKING WISE THE SIMPLE. THE STATUTES OF THE LORD ARE RIGHT, REJOICING THE HEART: THE COMMANDMENT OF THE LORD IS PURE, ENLIGHTENING THE EYES. THE FEAR OF THE LORD IS CLEAN, ENDURING FOR EVER: THE JUDGMENTS OF THE LORD ARE TRUE AND RIGHTEOUS ALTOGETHER. MORE TO BE DESIRED ARE THEY THAN GOLD, YEA, THAN MUCH FINE GOLD: SWEETER ALSO THAN HONEY AND THE HONEYCOMB. MOREOVER BY THEM IS THY SERVANT WARNED: AND IN KEEPING OF THEM THERE IS GREAT REWARD. PSALM 19:7-11

Good Morning!

We are counting down the days 'til Christmas! Are you getting excited? One of the reasons I like Christmas is all of the yummy things there are to eat! Like these sweet candies! I kind of got stuck trying to get some more. Oops!

Did you know that God's Word is sweet too? God's Word is to our souls like sweet food is to our tongues and bodies, a joy to savor. Psalm 34:8 says: "O taste and see that the Lord is good: blessed is the man that trusteth in him." and Psalm 19 talks about the commandments of the Lord being sweeter than honey!

I hope you enjoy this special sweet treat today, and every time you see these sweet candies I want you to remember that God's Word is sweet too!

Your Sweet Loving Friend, Melk

CREATE A PAPER MANGER SCENE

Promise

n. a declaration, written or verbal, made by one person to another, which binds the person who makes it, either in honor, conscience or law, to do or forbear a certain act specified.

MELK:

IS FOUND SITTING IN/ON THE MANGER SCENE, OR SITTING IN FRONT OF ONE CONTEMPLATIVELY

ACTIVITY:

CREATE YOUR OWN PAPER NATIVITY SCENE

MATERIALS:

SCISSORS, TAPE, CRAYONS, A PRINT OUT OF A PAPER MANGER SCENE. FIND ONE TO PRINT HERE:

WWW.MELKLINKS.COM

LESSON:

GOD PROMISED MESSIAH WOULD COME, AND HE DID!

SCRIPTURE:

AND THE ANGEL SAID UNTO THEM, FEAR NOT: FOR, BEHOLD, I BRING YOU GOOD TIDINGS OF GREAT JOY, WHICH SHALL BE TO ALL PEOPLE. FOR UNTO YOU IS BORN THIS DAY IN THE CITY OF DAVID A SAVIOUR, WHICH IS CHRIST THE LORD. AND THIS SHALL BE A SIGN UNTO YOU; YE SHALL FIND THE BABE WRAPPED IN SWADDLING CLOTHES, LYING IN A MANGER. LUKE 2:10-12

Good Morning!

I was just sitting here thinking about how God sent Jesus to earth as a baby. . . From the beginning of the world God knew he would do this and then he had someone record the story for us, so we can hear over and over again how God keeps his promises and provides salvation and pardon from our sins!

Can you imagine what it must have been like that night in the fields as the shepherds heard the angels and knew that God's promise had been fulfilled! I wish I could have been there! Luke 2:10-12 "And the angel said unto them, Fear not: for, behold, I bring you good tidings of great joy, which shall be to all people. For unto you is born this day in the city of David a Savior, which is Christ the Lord. And this shall be a sign unto you; Ye shall find the babe wrapped in swaddling clothes, lying in a manger."

Today, I have a manger scene for you to color and build out of paper! I want you to work together and have fun! And then you can use it to tell others the story of how God kept his promise!

Love, Melk

GOD GIVES GOOD GIFTS

Gift

n. A present; any thing given or bestowed; any thing, the property of which is voluntarily transferred by one person to another without compensation; a donation.

CANDY CANE WREATHS

MELK:

IS FOUND SITTING WITH CANDY CANES OR OTHER MATERIALS TRYING TO LAY THEM OUT FOR A WREATH

ACTIVITY:

MAKE CHRISTMAS WREATHS. GET INSTRUCTIONS HERE: WWW.MELKLINKS.COM, THEN, GIVE THEM AWAY TO FRIENDS, FAMILY OR NEIGHBORS.

MATERIALS:

CANDY CANES, (OR OTHER WREATH MATERIALS) GLUE, TAPE, SCISSORS, CARDBOARD, RIBBON, MARKERS

LESSON:

GOD GIVES GOOD GIFTS TO US WHETHER WE ARE GOOD OR BAD, BECAUSE HE LOVES US.

SCRIPTURE:

EVERY GOOD GIFT AND EVERY PERFECT GIFT IS FROM ABOVE, AND COMETH DOWN FROM THE FATHER OF LIGHTS, WITH WHOM IS NO VARIABLENESS, NEITHER SHADOW OF TURNING. JAMES 1:17

IF YE THEN, BEING EVIL, KNOW HOW TO GIVE GOOD GIFTS UNTO YOUR CHILDREN, HOW MUCH MORE SHALL YOUR FATHER WHICH IS IN HEAVEN GIVE GOOD THINGS TO THEM THAT ASK HIM? THEREFORE ALL THINGS WHATSOEVER YE WOULD THAT MEN SHOULD DO TO YOU, DO YE EVEN SO TO THEM: FOR THIS IS THE LAW AND THE PROPHETS. MATTHEW 7:11-12

Hi Guys!

Did you know that Santa says you have to be good girls and boys in order to get gifts at Christmas? But God is not that way. Listen to what the Bible says:

"Every good gift and every perfect gift is from above, and cometh down from the Father of lights, with whom is no variableness, neither shadow of turning." James 1:17

"If ye then, being evil, know how to give good gifts unto your children, how much more shall your Father which is in heaven give good things to them that ask him? Therefore all things whatsoever ye would that men should do to you, do ye even so to them: for this is the law and the prophets." Matthew 7:11-12

6   (continued on next page)

God says that HE gives us gifts because we are his children, it doesn't depend on what we do, because we could never be good enough to "earn" his love. He loves us because he is God! But he also says that we should give to others what we would like to receive, so today we're going to give a good gift to our neighbors. I laid out the instructions for you. Have fun!

Your Gift Loving Friend, Melk

GOD IS LIGHT

Light

n. That ethereal agent or matter which makes objects perceptible to the sense of seeing, but the particles of which are separately invisible.

CAMPOUT BY THE TREE

MELK:

IS FOUND SLEEPING IN FRONT OF THE CHRISTMAS TREE

ACTIVITY:

HAVE A CAMPOUT UNDER THE CHRISTMAS TREE

MATERIALS:

BLANKETS, PILLOWS ETC.

LESSON:

GOD IS LIGHT AND GIVES LIGHT TO THOSE IN DARKNESS.

SCRIPTURE:

GOD IS LIGHT, AND IN HIM IS NO DARKNESS AT ALL. 1 JOHN 1:5

WHICH THOU HAST PREPARED BEFORE THE FACE OF ALL PEOPLE; A LIGHT TO LIGHTEN THE GENTILES, AND THE GLORY OF THY PEOPLE ISRAEL. AND JOSEPH AND HIS MOTHER MARVELED AT THOSE THINGS WHICH WERE SPOKEN OF HIM. LUKE 2:31-33

Good Morning Friends!

I slept under your Christmas tree last night, looking at all the beautiful Christmas lights, and it reminded me about how God is light.

Did you know that the Bible says "God is light, and in him is no darkness at all" (1 John 1:5). And in Luke 2, the angel told Mary and Joseph that Jesus would be a light to bring salvation to the Gentiles (that's those people who are not Jews) and glory to Israel (the Jews).

Can you think of other ways that God is light to us?

For our fun activity today, your mom and dad said that we can plan a family camp out under the Christmas tree tonight! It's going to be so much fun to lay here and sing songs about Jesus and look at the lights, so get your sleeping bags out! I can't wait!

Your Light Loving Friend, Melk

HANG CHRISTMAS LIGHTS

Light
n. Illumination of mind; instruction; knowledge.

MELK:

IS FOUND UNTANGLING STRINGS OF CHRISTMAS LIGHTS

ACTIVITY:

DECORATE THE OUTSIDE OF YOUR HOUSE WITH CHRISTMAS LIGHTS, OR IF NOT THE OUTSIDE, HANG THEM FROM THE WALLS AND CEILINGS INSIDE OR IN YOUR BEDROOMS

MATERIALS:

CHRISTMAS LIGHTS

LESSON:

GOD GIVES US LIGHT TO SEE HIM FOR WHO HE IS AND TO BELIEVE HIM AND HE WILL MAKE US HIS CHILDREN.

SCRIPTURE:

IN HIM WAS LIFE; AND THE LIFE WAS THE LIGHT OF MEN. AND THE LIGHT SHINETH IN DARKNESS; AND THE DARKNESS COMPREHENDED IT NOT... THAT WAS THE TRUE LIGHT, WHICH LIGHTETH EVERY MAN THAT COMETH INTO THE WORLD. HE WAS IN THE WORLD, AND THE WORLD WAS MADE BY HIM, AND THE WORLD KNEW HIM NOT. HE CAME UNTO HIS OWN, AND HIS OWN RECEIVED HIM NOT. BUT AS MANY AS RECEIVED HIM, TO THEM GAVE HE POWER TO BECOME THE SONS OF GOD, EVEN TO THEM THAT BELIEVE ON HIS NAME.
JOHN 1:4-12

Hi Guys!

Don't you just love light! I love to look at them on the tree, and outside and everywhere!

God loves light too. In John 1 the Bible tell us that the life that we find in Christ is "the light of men", that He is the "true light" and that "to as many as received him, to them gave he power to become the sons of God, even to them that believe on his name."

Have you believed on God's name and become one of his children? If you haven't I want you to ask your mom or dad today, right now, about how you can become a child of God.

And then, lets have some fun hanging up these lights!

Your Enlightened Friend, Melk

GOD IS LIFE

Life

n. in man, that state of being in which the soul and body are united.

BIRTHDAY CELEBRATION

MELK:

IS FOUND WITH HAPPY BIRTHDAY SIGN/CARD/BALLOON/HATS, ETC.

ACTIVITY:

A FAMILY BIRTHDAY CELEBRATION

MATERIALS:

BIRTHDAY PARTY SUPPLIES. DOWNLOAD AND PRINT A FREE BIRTHDAY CARD FROM MELK HERE: WWW.MELKLINKS.COM

LESSON:

GOD IS THE GIVER AND SUSTAINER OF LIFE, BOTH PHYSICAL AND ETERNAL. (PARENTS, VISIT WWW.CANDYCANESFORLIFE.COM FOR HELPS IN EXPLAINING SALVATION AND ETERNAL LIFE TO CHILDREN.)

SCRIPTURE:

IN THE BEGINNING WAS THE WORD, AND THE WORD WAS WITH GOD, AND THE WORD WAS GOD. THE SAME WAS IN THE BEGINNING WITH GOD. ALL THINGS WERE MADE BY HIM; AND WITHOUT HIM WAS NOT ANY THING MADE THAT WAS MADE. IN HIM WAS LIFE; AND THE LIFE WAS THE LIGHT OF MEN. JOHN 1:1-4

FOR GOD SO LOVED THE WORLD, THAT HE GAVE HIS ONLY BEGOTTEN SON, THAT WHOSOEVER BELIEVETH IN HIM SHOULD NOT PERISH, BUT HAVE EVERLASTING LIFE. JOHN 3:16

THE SPIRIT OF GOD HATH MADE ME, AND THE BREATH OF THE ALMIGHTY HATH GIVEN ME LIFE. JOB 33:4

Happy Birthday to you! Happy Birthday to you! Happy Birthday from your Monkey! Happy Birthday to you!

Since today is _____'s birthday, I thought it would be the perfect day to remind you that God is the giver of life. God gave your parents life and he gave you life, and he continues to give all of us life each and every day with each breath we take.

And you know what else - when you got saved God also gave you eternal life! In John 1 the Bible says that God made all things! And in John 3:16 it tells us that he gives to those who believe on him eternal life and we will never die! If you haven't ever asked Jesus to forgive your sins, save you, and give you eternal life, why don't you talk to your Mom or Dad today and find out how to do that.

I hope you will have fun celebrating _____'s birthday today. Be sure to save a piece of cake for me!

Your Happy Friend, Melk

TELL THE GOSPEL STORY

Salvation
v. in theology, the redemption of man from the bondage of sin and liability to eternal death, and the conferring on him everlasting life.

MELK:

IS FOUND TELLING OR READING THE LEGEND OF THE CANDY CANE TO OTHER TOYS

ACTIVITY:

READ "THE CANDYMAKER'S GIFT: THE LEGEND OF THE CANDY CANE" TO FIND WHERE TO BUY THE BOOK, OR TO PRINT OUT THE LEGEND FROM ON ONLINE SOURCE VISIT: WWW.MELKLINKS.COM

MATERIALS:

DOWNLOADABLE STORY OR BOOK: "THE CANDYMAKER'S GIFT"

LESSON:

GOD IS SALVATION. (PARENTS VISIT WWW.CANDYCANESFORLIFE.COM FOR HELPS IN EXPLAINING SALVATION AND ETERNAL LIFE TO CHILDREN.)

SCRIPTURE:

FOR THE SON OF MAN IS COME TO SEEK AND TO SAVE THAT WHICH WAS LOST. LUKE 19:10

Hello There!

I was just sitting here reading the legend of the Candy Cane to some of my friends. Do you remember learning that God's Word is sweet? One of the sweetest things it tells us is that God is our Savior, and the candy cane can tell you the story of God's salvation!

In Luke 19:10 the Bible says that "the Son of Man" that's Jesus, "is come to seek and to save that which was lost." Like a shepherd searches for lost sheep. He came to find us, and to save us.

Have you asked Jesus to save you yet? Read the the story of the candy cane together today, and talk about the story, the candy, and about Jesus, our Savior. Then, be sure to tell the story to someone else too!

Your Candy Loving Friend, Melk

GOD IS ALL-POWERFUL (OMNIPOTENT)

Omnipotent

a. Almighty; possessing unlimited power; all powerful. The being that can create worlds must be omnipotent. Having unlimited power of a particular kind; as omnipotent love.

PAPER GINGERBREAD PEOPLE

MELK:

IS FOUND WITH A PAPER GINGERBREAD CUTOUT AND MARKERS

ACTIVITY:

MAKE LIFE-SIZE PAPER GINGERBREAD PEOPLE AND DECORATE

MATERIALS:

BUTCHER PAPER, POSTER BOARD, OR WRAPPING PAPER. TRACE OR DRAW A CHILD SIZE GINGERBREAD COOKIE. DECORATE WITH MARKERS, BUTTONS, BEADS OR OTHER DECORATIONS AS DESIRED.

LESSON:

GOD HAS POWER TO TRANSFORM AND TO MAKE NEW. HE CAN MAKE GOOD FROM BAD, BEAUTIFUL OUT OF UGLY, USEFUL OUT OF WORTHLESS.

SCRIPTURE:

THEREFORE IF ANY MAN BE IN CHRIST, HE IS A NEW CREATURE: OLD THINGS ARE PASSED AWAY; BEHOLD, ALL THINGS ARE BECOME NEW. 2 CORINTHIANS 5:17

HE HATH MADE EVERY THING BEAUTIFUL IN HIS TIME: ALSO HE HATH SET THE WORLD IN THEIR HEART, SO THAT NO MAN CAN FIND OUT THE WORK THAT GOD MAKETH FROM THE BEGINNING TO THE END. I KNOW THAT THERE IS NO GOOD IN THEM, BUT FOR A MAN TO REJOICE, AND TO DO GOOD IN HIS LIFE. AND ALSO THAT EVERY MAN SHOULD EAT AND DRINK, AND ENJOY THE GOOD OF ALL HIS LABOUR, IT IS THE GIFT OF GOD. I KNOW THAT, WHATSOEVER GOD DOETH, IT SHALL BE FOR EVER: NOTHING CAN BE PUT TO IT, NOR ANY THING TAKEN FROM IT: AND GOD DOETH IT, THAT MEN SHOULD FEAR BEFORE HIM. ECCLESIASTES 3:11-14

Happy Day to you all!

Did you know that God is omnipotent? That means all-powerful. God can transform the ugly things into beautiful things, (like caterpillars) and he can make good come from bad, and he can take old things and make them new. In 2 Corinthians 5:17 He tells us that when we get saved ALL things are become new! And in Ecclesiastes 3:11-14 He tells us that He makes everything beautiful in his time!

 (continued on next page)

Today, we're going to take some plain old paper and make it into beautiful Christmas decorations. You can trace your own shape as a reminder that God can make you a new person when you accept his free gift of salvation. Because he is all-powerful! Have fun!

Your Friend, Melk

GOD KEEPS HIS PROMISES

Promise

n. a declaration, written or verbal, made by one person to another, which binds the person who makes it, either in honor, conscience or law, to do or forbear a certain act specified.

CANDY CANE HUNT

MELK:

IS FOUND AFTER SUCCESSFULLY HIDING CANDY CANES ALL AROUND THE HOUSE

ACTIVITY:

HAVE A CANDY CANE HUNT

MATERIALS:

CANDY CANES

LESSON:

THOSE WHO SEEK HIM WILL FIND HIM.

SCRIPTURE:

I LOVE THEM THAT LOVE ME; AND THOSE THAT SEEK ME EARLY SHALL FIND ME. PROVERBS 8:17

AND YE SHALL SEEK ME, AND FIND ME, WHEN YE SHALL SEARCH FOR ME WITH ALL YOUR HEART. JEREMIAH 29:13

ASK, AND IT SHALL BE GIVEN YOU; SEEK, AND YE SHALL FIND; KNOCK, AND IT SHALL BE OPENED UNTO YOU: FOR EVERY ONE THAT ASKETH RECEIVETH; AND HE THAT SEEKETH FINDETH; AND TO HIM THAT KNOCKETH IT SHALL BE OPENED. MATTHEW 7:7-8

Hi Guys!

Wow! I've had a busy time! I've been working hard hiding something special for you to help you learn today's lesson!

Matthew 7:7-8 says "Ask, and it shall be given you; seek, and ye shall find; knock, and it shall be opened unto you: For every one that asketh receiveth; and he that seeketh findeth; and to him that knocketh it shall be opened."

God wants us to seek him, to ask him, to talk to him about our needs and our desires. And he promises to answer us. God always keeps his promises. We will find him if we seek him, just like you will find the candy canes I've hidden for you if you seek them.

Are you ready? Get set! Go!

Love, Melk

SURPRISE GIFTS

MELK:

IS FOUND AMIDST A PILE OF SMALL WRAPPED PRESENTS (ONE FOR EACH CHILD), SCRAPS OF WRAPPING PAPER AND RIBBONS

ACTIVITY:

OPEN AND ENJOY YOUR GIFTS FROM MELK

MATERIALS:

SCISSORS, TAPE, WRAPPING PAPER, SMALL GIFTS OR CANDY

LESSON:

GOD BLESSES US WHETHER WE ARE GOOD OR BAD, NOT BASED ON OUR GOODNESS, BUT ON HIS GOODNESS AND ON HIS LOVE FOR US.

SCRIPTURE:

FOR HE (GOD) MAKETH HIS SUN TO RISE ON THE EVIL AND ON THE GOOD, AND SENDETH RAIN ON THE JUST AND ON THE UNJUST. MATTHEW 5:45

GOD GIVES GOOD GIFTS

Good
a. Complete or sufficiently perfect in its kind; having the physical qualities best adapted to its design and use; opposed to bad, imperfect, corrupted, impaired.

Hi Guys!

I have another surprise for you today!

The Bible tells us that God "makes his sun to rise on the evil and on the good, and sends rain on the just and on the unjust" (Matthew 5:45). God doesn't bless us based on what we DO, but based on WHO HE is! Isn't that awesome! He loves us and blesses us because of his own goodness, whether we deserve it or not.

And whether you deserve it or not, because I love you, I have wrapped up some special surprise gifts for you today. I hope you will enjoy them and that they will help you remember how much God loves you even when you don't deserve it.

Your loving Friend, Melk

GOD IS A CONSUMING FIRE (A JEALOUS GOD)

Consuming

a. Completely expending; destroying in its entirety.

Jealous

a. Solicitous to defend the honor of; concerned for the character of. Suspiciously vigilant; anxiously careful and concerned for.

SMORES

MELK:

IS FOUND ROASTING A MARSHMALLOW OVER AN UNLIT CANDLE OR THE STOVE, WITH CHOCOLATE AND CRACKERS/COOKIES NEARBY

ACTIVITY:

MAKE SMORES TOGETHER

MATERIALS:

MARSHMALLOWS, CHOCOLATE, CRACKERS/COOKIES

LESSON:

GOD IS A JEALOUS GOD, HE WANTS ALL OF YOU, JUST AS THE FIRE IS NOT CONTENT TO HAVE PART OF THE MARSHMALLOW, BUT WANTS TO ENGULF IT ALL.

SCRIPTURE:

FOR THE LORD THY GOD IS A CONSUMING FIRE, EVEN A JEALOUS GOD. DEUTERONOMY 4:24

UNDERSTAND THEREFORE THIS DAY, THAT THE LORD THY GOD IS HE WHICH GOETH OVER BEFORE THEE; AS A CONSUMING FIRE HE SHALL DESTROY THEM, AND HE SHALL BRING THEM DOWN BEFORE THY FACE: SO SHALT THOU DRIVE THEM OUT, AND DESTROY THEM QUICKLY, AS THE LORD HATH SAID UNTO THEE. DEUTERONOMY 9:3

FOR OUR GOD IS A CONSUMING FIRE. HEBREWS 12:29

Good morning!

Today I want to invite you to make smores together! It's a sticky mess, but it's yummy!

Did you know that God is like the fire?

The Bible actually says that God is a consuming fire. (Deuteronomy 4:24) Just like the fire wants to consume all of the marshmallow, God is a jealous God and wants all of us. He doesn't want to share us, our worship, or our service with anyone else.

But God is also Jelous in that he wants to defend and be concerned for his own honor. Everything you do is reflection to others of what God is like. While you make your smores, talk about how you can be careful to defend God's honor today.

BAKE GINGERBREAD COOKIES

Life

n. in man, that state of being in which the soul and body are united.

MELK:

IS FOUND HUGGING A GINGERBREAD MAN COOKIE CUTTER, RECIPE AND INGREDIENTS OR READING "THE GINGERBREAD BOY"

ACTIVITY:

MAKE GINGERBREAD COOKIES. FIND LINKS TO THE GINGERBREAD COOKIE RECIPE, THE BOOK "THE GINGERBREAD BOY", OR TO READ THE STORY ONLINE AT:

WWW.MELKLINKS.COM

(OPTIONAL: READ BOOK: "THE GINGERBREAD BOY")

MATERIALS:

BAKING SUPPLIES AND UTENSILS, (OPTIONAL BOOK: "THE GINGERBREAD BOY")

LESSON:

GOD IS THE CREATOR OF MAN AND BREATHES LIFE INTO HIM.

SCRIPTURE:

AND THE LORD GOD FORMED MAN OF THE DUST OF THE GROUND, AND BREATHED INTO HIS NOSTRILS THE BREATH OF LIFE; AND MAN BECAME A LIVING SOUL. GENESIS 2:7

Good morning!

Do you remember how I told you that God is all-powerful (omnipotent) and he can turn ugly things into beautiful ones. Well, God can also create life!

In Genesis 2:7 The Bible tell us that "the Lord God formed man of the dust of the ground, and breathed into his nostrils the breath of life; and man became a living soul". That man was Adam, who was the father of all living people today. And we are still living because God continues to give us breath. Every moment of every day is a gift of life from God.

To remind us of how God made man from the ground, we are going to make gingerbread men from cookie dough today! It's going to be so much fun! Go wash your hands and find an apron and let's get busy!

Your Life Loving Friend, Melk

GOD IS CREATOR (AND CREATIVE)

Creator

n. The being or person that creates.

Creative

a. Having the power to create, or exerting the act of creation; as creative fancy; creative power.

PAPER SNOWFLAKES

MELK:

IS FOUND WITH SCISSORS IN HAND CUTTING OUT PAPER SNOWFLAKES (OPTIONAL BOOK NEARBY)

ACTIVITY:

MAKE PAPER SNOWFLAKES. YOU CAN FIND LINKS TO THE SNOWFLAKE TEMPLATES, OR BOOK: "SNOWFLAKE BENTLY" HERE: WWW.MELKLINKS.COM

(OPTIONAL - HANG THEM FROM THE CEILING)

(OPTIONAL - READ BOOK: "SNOWFLAKE BENTLY")

MATERIALS:

PAPER, SCISSORS, STRING (OPTIONAL BOOK: "SNOWFLAKE BENTLY)

LESSON:

GOD MAKES ALL THINGS DISTINCT, UNIQUE AND BEAUTIFUL, NO TWO ALIKE EVER.

SCRIPTURE:

HE HATH MADE EVERY THING BEAUTIFUL IN HIS TIME. ECCLESIASTES 3:11A

ALL THINGS WERE MADE BY HIM (GOD); AND WITHOUT HIM WAS NOT ANY THING MADE THAT WAS MADE. JOHN 1:3

Hello everyone!

Don't you just love the snowflakes I've been making? Do you like snow? I do. And God does too. Did you know that scientists who have studied snow have never ever found two snowflakes exactly the same!

The Bible says that "All things were made by [God]; and without him was not any thing made that was made" (John 1:3). And that "He hath made every thing beautiful in his time" (Ecclesiastes 3:11a).

Today you're going to (read Snowflake Bently and) make some snowflakes of your own to hang around your Christmas Tree. And as you make them I want you to praise your Creator God for his creativity and for the beauty of his creation.

Your Friend, Melk

TEST YOUR KNOWLEDGE

MELK:

IS FOUND PLAYING A BIBLE TRIVIA GAME, PERHAPS WITH OTHER TOYS

ACTIVITY:

PLAY A BIBLE TRIVIA GAME TOGETHER. IF YOU DON'T HAVE ONE, YOU CAN PLAY ONLINE OR DOWNLOAD GAME PRINTABLES AND QUESTIONS AT: WWW.MELKLINKS.COM

MATERIALS:

BIBLE TRIVIA GAME

LESSON:

GOD KNOWS EVERYTHING. HE IS INFINITELY WISER AND MORE KNOWLEDGEABLE THAN WE.

SCRIPTURE:

HE TELLETH THE NUMBER OF THE STARS; HE CALLETH THEM ALL BY THEIR NAMES. PSALM 147:4

BUT THE VERY HAIRS OF YOUR HEAD ARE ALL NUMBERED. MATTHEW 10:30

FOR THE WORD OF GOD IS QUICK, AND POWERFUL, AND SHARPER THAN ANY TWO EDGED SWORD, PIERCING EVEN TO THE DIVIDING ASUNDER OF SOUL AND SPIRIT, AND OF THE JOINTS AND MARROW, AND IS A DISCERNER OF THE THOUGHTS AND INTENTS OF THE HEART. HEBREWS 4:12

GOD IS ALL-KNOWING (OMNISCIENT)

Omniscient
a. Having universal knowledge or knowledge of all things; infinitely knowing; all-seeing; as the omniscient God.

Hello again!

If you were omniscient like God (that means knowing everything) you would know I've been practicing up on my Bible knowledge. I don't know everything like God does, so I have been reviewing with my friend.

God is so smart, the Bible says that he knows "the number of the stars, and calls them all by their names" (Psalm 147:4) and that "Even the very hairs of your head are all numbered" (Mathtew 10:30). And what's more Hebrews 4:12 tells us that God even knows the thoughts of our hearts! The things we don't even say out loud! That is amazing knowledge!

(continued on next page)

Today, you get to play a Bible trivia game together to review your Bible knowledge and to learn some new things. It's going to be fun! Who wants to be on my team?

Your Knowledge Loving Friend, Melk

STAR ORNAMENTS

MELK:

IS FOUND SITTING IN CHRISTMAS TREE LOOKING UP AT THE STAR OR SITTING AMID ALL OF THE CRAFT SUPPLIES TRYING TO MAKE A STAR

ACTIVITY:

MAKE STAR ORNAMENTS. FIND CRAFT INSTRUCTIONS AND LINKS TO THE DOCUMENTARY AT:

WWW.MELKLINKS.COM

(OPTIONAL: WATCH THE "STAR OF BETHLEHEM" DOCUMENTARY)

MATERIALS:

PIPE CLEANERS AND CRAFT BEADS

(OPTIONAL: "STAR OF BETHLEHEM" DOCUMENTARY)

LESSON:

GOD IS A POWERFUL CREATOR WHO MADE THE STARS AND PUT THEM IN SPACE TO ACCOMPLISH HIS PURPOSES.

SCRIPTURE:

AND GOD SAID, LET THERE BE LIGHTS IN THE FIRMAMENT OF THE HEAVEN TO DIVIDE THE DAY FROM THE NIGHT; AND LET THEM BE FOR SIGNS, AND FOR SEASONS, AND FOR DAYS, AND YEARS: AND LET THEM BE FOR LIGHTS IN THE FIRMAMENT OF THE HEAVEN TO GIVE LIGHT UPON THE EARTH: AND IT WAS SO. AND GOD MADE TWO GREAT LIGHTS; THE GREATER LIGHT TO RULE THE DAY, AND THE LESSER LIGHT TO RULE THE NIGHT: HE MADE THE STARS ALSO. AND GOD SET THEM IN THE FIRMAMENT OF THE HEAVEN TO GIVE LIGHT UPON THE EARTH, AND TO RULE OVER THE DAY AND OVER THE NIGHT, AND TO DIVIDE THE LIGHT FROM THE DARKNESS: AND GOD SAW THAT IT WAS GOOD.DARKNESS: AND GOD SAW THAT IT WAS GOOD. GENESIS 1:14-18

GOD IS CREATOR (AND CREATIVE)

Creator

n. The being or person that creates.

Creative

a. Having the power to create, or exerting the act of creation; as creative fancy; creative power.

Good Morning!

Can you guess what I'm doing? Have you ever thought about the stars? How big are they really? How many are there? How do they shine and stay where they are not explode or crash or...?

(continued on next page)

In Genesis 1, the Bible says that God made the sun, moon and stars and "divided the day from the night; and let them be for signs, and for seasons, and for days, and years: And let them be for lights in the firmament of the heaven to give light upon the earth" and that it was good, not to mention beautiful! God also used the stars to guide the wise men to the Christ child. What an awesome Creator God we have!

And because we were made in his image, we also enjoy creating things. Today, we get to create star ornaments to remind us of our Creator God and his wonderful lights in the sky!

Your Creative Friend, Melk

BE AN ARTIST

MELK:

SPELLING OUT "HAPPY" OR MAKING ART WITH CEREAL (OR RICE, BEANS, LENTILS, MARSHMALLOWS, NOODLES, ETC.) OR PAINTING A PICTURE WITH PAINTS

ACTIVITY:

MAKE CHRISTMAS ART OR WORD ART (MAYBE TO GIVE AS A GIFT) FIND EXAMPLES AND IDEAS AT:

WWW.MELKLINKS.COM

MATERIALS:

PAPER, GLUE, CEREAL, RICE, BEANS, LENTILS, MARSHMALLOWS, NOODLES, PAINT, MARKERS, ETC.

LESSON:

GOD TAKES PLEASURE IN HIS CREATION.

SCRIPTURE:

THOU ART WORTHY, O LORD, TO RECEIVE GLORY AND HONOUR AND POWER: FOR THOU HAST CREATED ALL THINGS, AND FOR THY PLEASURE THEY ARE AND WERE CREATED. REVELATION 4:11

Pleasure

n. The gratification of the senses or of the mind; agreeable sensations or emotions; the excitement, relish or happiness produced by enjoyment or the expectation of good; opposed to pain.

Hi Friend!

Remember how we talked about God creating the stars? That wasn't the only thing he created? In fact, in Revelation, God tells us that he "created all things"! That means you and me too. And it also tells us that we were created for his pleasure!

"Thou art worthy, O Lord, to receive glory and honour and power: for thou hast created all things, and for thy pleasure they are and were created." Revelation 4:11

Do you get pleasure from creating too? What about when you create something and give it as a gift to someone else? Does that give you pleasure? Today we're going to enjoy creating some works of art, using other things God has created. And if you'd like to, you can give it away to someone when you are finished.

Have fun! And don't forget to clean up your mess!

Love, Melk

GOD IS EVERYWHERE (OMNIPRESENT)

Omnipresent

a. Present in all places at the same time; as the omnipresent Jehovah.

TAKE A TRIP

NOTE: TODAY'S ACTIVITY IS A GOOD ONE TO DO WITH A SURPRISE TRIP SOMEWHERE FOR THE HOLIDAYS. LET MELK ANNOUNCE IT TO THE FAMILY!

MELK:

IS FOUND PACKING HIS SUITCASE OR SITTING IN/ON TOP OF A PACKED SUITCASE WITH MAPS/TICKETS, ETC.

ACTIVITY:

TAKE A TRIP ACROSS TOWN OR ACROSS THE WORLD

MATERIALS:

SUITCASE, TRAVEL PROPS, TICKETS, ETC.

LESSON:

GOD IS EVERYWHERE ALL AT THE SAME TIME.

SCRIPTURE:

WHITHER SHALL I GO FROM THY SPIRIT? OR WHITHER SHALL I FLEE FROM THY PRESENCE? IF I ASCEND UP INTO HEAVEN, THOU ART THERE: IF I MAKE MY BED IN HELL, BEHOLD, THOU ART THERE. IF I TAKE THE WINGS OF THE MORNING, AND DWELL IN THE UTTERMOST PARTS OF THE SEA; EVEN THERE SHALL THY HAND LEAD ME, AND THY RIGHT HAND SHALL HOLD ME. PSALM 139:7-10

FOR HE HATH SAID, I WILL NEVER LEAVE THEE, NOR FORSAKE THEE. HEBREWS 13:5B

Hello everyone!

I have been excitedly waiting and preparing for today!

Do you know where _____ (destination) _____ is? Do you know that God is there right now? And he is here right now too! That is because God is so big and so powerful that he can be everywhere all at the same time.

In the Bible God says " I will never leave thee, nor forsake thee." Hebrews 13:5b, and that we cannot outrun God. No matter where we go, he is there. (Psalm 139:7-10)

I hope you're as excited as I am about our trip to ___ (destination)_____! It's going to be so much fun! Don't forget to look for things that remind you of who God is as you travel. And don't be afraid, because he is with you and he is already at your destination too! Happy Travels!

Your Traveling Friend, Melk

GIFTS FOR THE HARD-TO-LOVE

Good
a. Complete or sufficiently perfect in its kind; having the physical qualities best adapted to its design and use; opposed to bad, imperfect, corrupted, impaired.

MELK:

IS FOUND WRAPPING PRESENTS. PERHAPS A PIECE OF CANDY OR A SMALL TOY OR OTHER GIFTS

ACTIVITY:

WRAP GIFTS FOR CHILDREN YOU DON'T LIKE AND DELIVER THEM WITH A CHRISTMAS CARD.

MATERIALS:

SCISSORS, TAPE, WRAPPING PAPER, SMALL GIFTS OR CANDY, CHRISTMAS CARDS (PARENTS MIGHT NEED TO HELP HERE IN HAVING GIFTS PURCHASED AHEAD OF TIME AND PEOPLE IN MIND TO BE KIND TO. YOU MIGHT ALSO WANT TO GIVE THEM A TRACT.) YOU CAN DOWNLOAD AND PRINT CHRISTMAS CARDS AND TRACTS HERE: WWW.MELKLINKS.COM

LESSON:

GOD LOVES EVEN THOSE WHO HATE HIM, CURSE HIM AND PERSECUTE HIM.

SCRIPTURE:

YE HAVE HEARD THAT IT HATH BEEN SAID, THOU SHALT LOVE THY NEIGHBOUR, AND HATE THINE ENEMY. BUT I SAY UNTO YOU, LOVE YOUR ENEMIES, BLESS THEM THAT CURSE YOU, DO GOOD TO THEM THAT HATE YOU, AND PRAY FOR THEM WHICH DESPITEFULLY USE YOU, AND PERSECUTE YOU; THAT YE MAY BE THE CHILDREN OF YOUR FATHER WHICH IS IN HEAVEN: FOR HE MAKETH HIS SUN TO RISE ON THE EVIL AND ON THE GOOD, AND SENDETH RAIN ON THE JUST AND ON THE UNJUST. FOR IF YE LOVE THEM WHICH LOVE YOU, WHAT REWARD HAVE YE? DO NOT EVEN THE PUBLICANS THE SAME? AND IF YE SALUTE YOUR BRETHREN ONLY, WHAT DO YE MORE THAN OTHERS? DO NOT EVEN THE PUBLICANS SO? BE YE THEREFORE PERFECT, EVEN AS YOUR FATHER WHICH IS IN HEAVEN IS PERFECT. BE YE THEREFORE PERFECT, EVEN AS YOUR FATHER WHICH IS IN HEAVEN IS PERFECT. MATTHEW 5:43-48

Hi Guys!

Today's lesson might be kind of hard to learn, but it's important if we are to know God and understand how he loves.

(continued on next page)

Do you remember we learned that God loves us because of WHO HE is, and not because of what we do? Can you think of someone you know who you really, really don't like? God loves them too, and says we are to bless them, and do good to them. Pray for them, and love them (Matthew 5:43-48). Because whether they deserve it or not, God loves them, and wants us to show them his love through his good gifts.

Today, we're going to wrap some gifts and deliver them to those hard-to-love people, and we're going to pray for them to accept God's love.

Your Loving Friend, Melk

FUNNY PHOTOS

Joy

n. The passion or emotion excited by the acquisition or expectation of good; a delight of the mind, from the consideration of the present or assured approaching possession of a good.

MELK:

IS FOUND WITH PHOTO PROPS AND CAMERA

ACTIVITY:

TAKE FUNNY PHOTOS

MATERIALS:

PHOTO PROPS (HATS, SCARVES, GLASSES, MUSTACHE, COSTUMES, ETC) AND CAMERA. IF YOU DON'T HAVE PHOTO PROPS, GO HERE TO FIND IDEAS AND LINKS TO DOWNLOADABLE ONES YOU CAN MAKE YOURSELF: WWW.MELKLINKS.COM

LESSON:

GOD LIKES US TO BE JOYFUL.

SCRIPTURE:

A MERRY HEART DOETH GOOD LIKE A MEDICINE: BUT A BROKEN SPIRIT DRIETH THE BONES. PROVERBS 17:22

Hi Guys!

Are you joyful today? Did you know that God likes us to be joyful? And that it is healthy for us?

Proverbs 17:22 says "A merry heart doeth good like a medicine: but a broken spirit drieth the bones." When was the last time you laughed together with your family?

Today I want you to find joy in doing something silly with each other. We're going to take some silly photos so we can laugh together at how silly we look. I've collected some things you can use and you can make some more of your own silly props too, if you want to. Have fun!

Your Joyful Friend, Melk

GOD IS A MIRACLE WORKING GOD

Miracle

n. a wonder or wonderful thing.

n. In theology, an event or effect contrary to the established constitution and course of things, or a deviation from the known laws of nature. Miracles can be wrought only by Almighty power, as when Christ healed lepers, saying, "I will, be thou clean," or calmed the tempest, "Peace, be still."

MIRACLES

NOTE: FOR THIS ACTIVITY YOU CAN CHOOSE A MORE SCIENTIFIC ROUTE IF YOU HAVE THE RESOURCES AVAILABLE IN YOUR SEASON, OR AN IMAGINATIVE ONE.

MELK:

SCIENTIFIC: IS FOUND WATCHING A CATERPILLAR/ FISH TANK OR IN A PILE OF BEANS/SEEDS

IMAGINARY: IS FOUND "PLANTING" HERSHEY KISSES, PEPPERMINTS OR OTHER SMALL CANDIES IN A CUP OR SMALL POT FULL OF DIRT OR SUGAR

ACTIVITY:

SCIENTIFIC: WATCH BUTTERFLIES HATCH FROM COCOONS, FISH HATCH FROM EGGS, OR WATCH PLANTS GROW FROM BEANS OR OTHER SEEDS. FIND LINKS TO PURCHASE A BUTTERFLY GARDEN AT WWW.MELKLINKS.COM

IMAGINARY: PLANT THE CANDIES AND WATCH AS THE NEXT DAY THEY GROW INTO MINIATURE CANDY BARS OR MINIATURE CANDY CANES (PARENTS SWITCH THEM OUT WHEN KIDS AREN'T LOOKING) AND THE NEXT DAY INTO FULL SIZED CANDY BARS OR CANDY CANES THAT CAN BE "HARVESTED" AND EATEN.

MATERIALS:

SCIENTIFIC: CATERPILLARS AND BUTTERFLY HOUSE, FISH TANK AND EGGS, SEEDS, ETC, DEPENDING ON WHAT YOU DECIDE TO USE.

IMAGINARY: CANDIES, CUP OR POT OF DIRT OR SUGAR

LESSON:

GOD HAS POWER TO DO MIRACLES.

SCRIPTURE:

BUT THOUGH HE HAD DONE SO MANY MIRACLES BEFORE THEM, YET THEY BELIEVED NOT ON HIM: JOHN 12:37

BUT JESUS BEHELD THEM, AND SAID UNTO THEM, WITH MEN THIS IS IMPOSSIBLE; BUT WITH GOD ALL THINGS ARE POSSIBLE.

Well, hello there!

Do you see what I'm watching? I am waiting for a miracle, for God to turn it into something else.

(continued on next page)

Do you believe God has all power? Do you believe he can do miracles? The Bible talks about many miracles that Jesus did when he was here on earth, but God continues to work miracles even today! Can you think of some miracles that God has done? (answers may vary: snow, leaves changing color, Grandma's hair changing to silver, someone getting better when they are sick, etc.)

I want you to help me plant/watch this and over the next few days lets see what kind of miracle God will do.

Your Excited, but trying to be patient Friend, Melk

GOD IS MUSICAL

Praise

n. Commendation bestowed on a person for his personal virtues or worthy actions, on meritorious actions themselves, or on any thing valuable; approbation expressed in words or song.

CHRISTMAS CONCERT

MELK:

IS FOUND HOLDING TICKETS OR A PLAYBILL/ADVERTISEMENT FOR A CHRISTMAS CONCERT.

ACTIVITY:

ATTEND A CHRISTMAS CONCERT TOGETHER

MATERIALS:

TICKETS, PLAYBILL, ADVERTISEMENT ETC.

LESSON:

GOD LOVES FOR US TO PRAISE HIM IN MUSIC.

SCRIPTURE:

PRAISE YE THE LORD. PRAISE GOD IN HIS SANCTUARY: PRAISE HIM IN THE FIRMAMENT OF HIS POWER. PRAISE HIM FOR HIS MIGHTY ACTS: PRAISE HIM ACCORDING TO HIS EXCELLENT GREATNESS. PRAISE HIM WITH THE SOUND OF THE TRUMPET: PRAISE HIM WITH THE PSALTERY AND HARP. PRAISE HIM WITH THE TIMBREL AND DANCE: PRAISE HIM WITH STRINGED INSTRUMENTS AND ORGANS. PRAISE HIM UPON THE LOUD CYMBALS: PRAISE HIM UPON THE HIGH SOUNDING CYMBALS. LET EVERY THING THAT HATH BREATH PRAISE THE LORD. PRAISE YE THE LORD. PSALM 150:1-6

Do, Re, Mi, Fa, So, La, Ti...

Oh, hi! I was just practicing my singing.

Don't you love it when people sing to you? Did you know that God loves it when we sing to him too! You did? Well then, you must know that God is musical. He created music, and he gives us our musical abilities, and he loves it when we praise him and sing to him.

I am so excited that we will get to go to a Christmas concert today and praise God and enjoy music together!

Get your best concert clothes ready and go warm up your singing voice. It's praise time!

Your Singing Friend, Melk

NEW CHRISTMAS MUSIC

Music

n. Melody or harmony; any succession of sounds so modulated as to please the ear, or any combination of simultaneous sounds in accordance or harmony. Music is vocal or instrumental.

MELK:

IS FOUND HOLDING A NEW CD AND/OR WITH IPOD HEADPHONES IN "LISTENING" TO MUSIC

ACTIVITY:

ENJOY LISTENING TO A NEW CD, OR CHRISTMAS MUSIC DOWNLOAD TOGETHER. GO HERE FOR LINKS TO SOME OF MELK'S FAVORITE CHRISTMAS SONGS: WWW.MELKLINKS.COM

MATERIALS:

NEW CD (OR ONE YOU HAVEN'T LISTENED TO IN A WHILE) YOUR IPOD/RADIO AND HEADPHONES

LESSON:

GOD GIVES US MUSIC AS WAY TO GIVE US JOY.

SCRIPTURE:

THEREFORE THE REDEEMED OF THE LORD SHALL RETURN, AND COME WITH SINGING UNTO ZION; AND EVERLASTING JOY SHALL BE UPON THEIR HEAD: THEY SHALL OBTAIN GLADNESS AND JOY; AND SORROW AND MOURNING SHALL FLEE AWAY. ISAIAH 51:11

La, la, la, la, la, la, la!

Oh, hello. I didn't hear you coming. I was singing/listening to these songs. They're so pretty!

In the Bible God puts singing and joy together. Listen to this: "Therefore the redeemed of the Lord shall return, and come with singing unto Zion; and everlasting joy shall be upon their head: they shall obtain gladness and joy; and sorrow and mourning shall flee away" (Isaiah 51:11).

Isn't it cool that when we feel bad or down in the dumps we can sing to the Lord and begin to feel better! You should try it! Enjoy your (new) music today and enjoy singing along when you can and see how it gives you joy.

Your Musical Friend, Melk

GOD IS MUSICAL

Carol

n. A song of joy and exultation; a song of devotion; or a song in general.

Caroling

v. To sing; to warble; to sing in joy or festivity.

GO CAROLING

MELK:

IS FOUND LOOKING THROUGH A SONGBOOK OR BOOK OF CHRISTMAS HYMNS OR A PRINT OUT OF A CHRISTMAS SONG

ACTIVITY:

GO CAROLING

MATERIALS:

SONG BOOKS, OR PRINT OUTS OF CHRISTMAS SONGS. IF YOU NEED TO PURCHASE A SONGBOOK, OR A MUSIC DOWNLOAD, GO HERE TO FIND LINKS TO MELK'S FAVORITES:

WWW.MELKLINKS.COM

LESSON:

GOD LOVES FOR US TO PRAISE HIM IN MUSIC.

SCRIPTURE:

O SING UNTO THE LORD A NEW SONG: SING UNTO THE LORD, ALL THE EARTH. SING UNTO THE LORD, BLESS HIS NAME; SHEW FORTH HIS SALVATION FROM DAY TO DAY. DECLARE HIS GLORY AMONG THE HEATHEN, HIS WONDERS AMONG ALL PEOPLE. FOR THE LORD IS GREAT, AND GREATLY TO BE PRAISED: HE IS TO BE FEARED ABOVE ALL GODS. FOR ALL THE GODS OF THE NATIONS ARE IDOLS: BUT THE LORD MADE THE HEAVENS. HONOUR AND MAJESTY ARE BEFORE HIM: STRENGTH AND BEAUTY ARE IN HIS SANCTUARY. GIVE UNTO THE LORD, O YE KINDREDS OF THE PEOPLE, GIVE UNTO THE LORD GLORY AND STRENGTH. GIVE UNTO THE LORD THE GLORY DUE UNTO HIS NAME: BRING AN OFFERING, AND COME INTO HIS COURTS. O WORSHIP THE LORD IN THE BEAUTY OF HOLINESS: FEAR BEFORE HIM, ALL THE EARTH. SAY AMONG THE HEATHEN THAT THE LORD REIGNETH: THE WORLD ALSO SHALL BE ESTABLISHED THAT IT SHALL NOT BE MOVED: HE SHALL JUDGE THE PEOPLE RIGHTEOUSLY. PSALM 96:1-10

Hi Guys!

Remember how God created all things, how he loves music and wants us to praise him and that singing can bring joy?

26   (continued on next page)

Listen to what God says in Psalm 96: "O sing unto the Lord a new song: sing unto the Lord, all the earth. Sing unto the Lord, bless his name; shew forth his salvation from day to day. Declare his glory among the heathen, his wonders among all people. For the Lord is great, and greatly to be praised" (vs. 1-4).

Today, we're going to show forth his salvation and declare his glory to others by singing songs of Christmas! Grab your songbooks friends, and let's go caroling!

Your Joyful Friend, Melk

GOD IS OUR GOOD PROVIDER

Good

a. Complete or sufficiently perfect in its kind; having the physical qualities best adapted to its design and use; opposed to bad, imperfect, corrupted, impaired.

Provider

n. One who provides, furnishes or supplies; one that procures what is wanted.

Good Morning!

MAKE A FRUIT PIE

MELK:

IS FOUND LOOKING AT PIE RECIPES, HUGGING A RECIPE BOX WITH CHOSEN RECIPE STICKING OUT OBVIOUSLY, IN A PILE OF FRUIT OR WITH A PILE OF PIE MAKING INGREDIENTS AND UTENSILS

ACTIVITY:

MAKE A FRUIT PIE TOGETHER. YOU CAN FIND SOME OF MELK'S FAVORITE PIE RECIPES AT:

WWW.MELKLINKS.COM

MATERIALS:

PIE MAKING INGREDIENTS AND UTENSILS

LESSON:

GOD IS OUR GOOD PROVIDER.

SCRIPTURE:

BUT MY GOD SHALL SUPPLY ALL YOUR NEED ACCORDING TO HIS RICHES IN GLORY BY CHRIST JESUS. PHILIPPIANS 4:19

ACCORDING AS HIS DIVINE POWER HATH GIVEN UNTO US ALL THINGS THAT PERTAIN UNTO LIFE AND GODLINESS, THROUGH THE KNOWLEDGE OF HIM THAT HATH CALLED US TO GLORY AND VIRTUE. 2 PETER 1:3

THE LORD IS MY SHEPHERD. I SHALL NOT WANT. PSALM 23:1

FOR THE LORD GOD IS A SUN AND SHIELD: THE LORD WILL GIVE GRACE AND GLORY: NO GOOD THING WILL HE WITHHOLD FROM THEM THAT WALK UPRIGHTLY. PSALM 84:11

AND OUT OF THE GROUND MADE THE LORD GOD TO GROW EVERY TREE THAT IS PLEASANT TO THE SIGHT, AND GOOD FOR FOOD; THE TREE OF LIFE ALSO IN THE MIDST OF THE GARDEN, AND THE TREE OF KNOWLEDGE OF GOOD AND EVIL. GENESIS 2:9

Did you know that one way God takes care of us is by providing for all of our needs.

In Genesis 2:9 the Bible tells us that God made plants and trees that are good for food. And in 2 Peter 1:3 it says that God has "given unto us all things that pertain unto life and godliness, through the knowledge of him that hath called us to glory and virtue."

(continued on next page)

But it gets even better! Remember how God gives us good gifts? In Psalm 84:11 he also promises not to "withhold any good thing from those who walk uprightly" (righteously).

God is our good provider. As you make a pie today, talk about the other ways God has provided for your needs. What good things has God given you that you can thank him for?

Your Pie Loving Friend, Melk

Strong

a. Having physical passive power; having ability to bear or endure; firm; solid. Well fortified; able to sustain attacks; not easily subdued or taken; as a strong fortress or town.

BUILD A GINGERBREAD HOUSE

MELK:

IS FOUND WITH GINGERBREAD HOUSE BUILDING SUPPLIES

ACTIVITY:

BUILD A GINGERBREAD HOUSE TOGETHER. IF YOU'VE NEVER DONE IT YOU CAN PURCHASE KITS, SEE DECORATING IDEAS OR DOWNLOAD RECIPES AND INSTRUCTIONS HERE: WWW.MELKLINKS.COM

MATERIALS:

GINGERBREAD OR GRAHAM CRACKERS, FROSTING, CANDIES

LESSON:

GOD IS THE ONE ON WHOSE TRUTH AND PRINCIPLES WE SHOULD BUILD. HIS TRUTH WILL PROVIDE PROTECTION.

SCRIPTURE:

THE GOD OF MY ROCK; IN HIM WILL I TRUST: HE IS MY SHIELD, AND THE HORN OF MY SALVATION, MY HIGH TOWER, AND MY REFUGE, MY SAVIOUR; THOU SAVEST ME FROM VIOLENCE. 2 SAMUEL 22:3

MATTHEW 7 – THE STORY OF THE WISE AND FOOLISH MAN

Hi Guys!

Are you ready for some fun? I've been sitting here trying to think like an architect and decide how to build this Gingerbread house. I know it needs a firm foundation so that it won't fall. Do you think we should build it on a paper plate or a glass one?

You know, the Bible talks about God being our builder, and our rock, or foundation, to protect us, and in Matthew 7 he tells the story of the wise man and foolish man. The wise man built his house on the rock, the strong foundation, and when the storms came, his house withstood the storm. If you haven't read it, it's a great story! God is like a rock too. If we build our lives around his principles, when the storms of life come, he will help us weather them in a way that brings Him glory.

Talk about that as you help me build this house today. How is God strong for you? How does he protect you? How does knowing who he is help you through the hard times?

PASS OUT TRACKS

Salvation
v. in theology, the redemption of man from the bondage of sin and liability to eternal death, and the conferring on him everlasting life.

MELK:

IS FOUND SITTING ON OR HOLDING A PILE OF TRACTS

ACTIVITY:

PASS OUT TRACTS TO NEIGHBORS, FRIENDS, AND/OR AS AN OUTREACH IN YOUR TOWN OR WITH YOUR CHURCH

(OPTIONAL: GIVE AWAY TRACTS WITH CANDY/BAKED GOODS, ORNAMENTS OR OTHER SMALL GIFTS)

MATERIALS:

TRACTS, IF YOU DON'T HAVE ANY, YOU CAN PRINT SOME HERE: WWW.MELKLINKS.COM

OPTIONAL: CANDY, BAKED GOODS, ORNAMENTS OR OTHER SMALL GIFTS

LESSON:

GOD LOVES EVERYONE AND WANTS EVERY PERSON TO HAVE A CHANCE TO HEAR THE GOSPEL AND ACCEPT HIS SALVATION.

SCRIPTURE:

THE LORD IS NOT SLACK CONCERNING HIS PROMISE, AS SOME MEN COUNT SLACKNESS; BUT IS LONGSUFFERING TO US-WARD, NOT WILLING THAT ANY SHOULD PERISH, BUT THAT ALL SHOULD COME TO REPENTANCE. 2 PETER 3:9

Well, Hello there!

Christmas is getting closer! I am so excited to celebrate the birth of our Savior, aren't you? How many days are left?

Did you know that one of the greatest gifts a person can give to another person is to tell him about Jesus and his gift of salvation and forgiveness from sins? In 2 Peter 3:9, God tells us that he doesn't want anyone to perish, but wants all men to come to repentance.

Today, we get to be the hands and feet of Jesus, taking the news of salvation, the greatest gift God has to offer, to our friends and neighbors.

Your Gift Loving Friend, Melk

GOD'S WORD IS TRUTH

Truth

n. Conformity to fact or reality; exact accordance with that which is, or has been, or shall be. The true state of facts or things.

READ THE STORY OF THE FIRST CHRISTMAS

MELK:

IS FOUND WITH HIS BIBLE OPEN TO LUKE 2 OR A PICTURE BOOK OF THE CHRISTMAS STORY

ACTIVITY:

READ THE CHRISTMAS STORY TOGETHER

(OPTIONAL: READ BOOK: "THE VERY FIRST CHRISTMAS")

MATERIALS:

A BIBLE,

(OPTIONAL BOOK: "THE VERY FIRST CHRISTMAS".) TO FIND WHERE TO BUY THE BOOK , OR TO READ THE STORY ONLINE, VISIT:

WWW.MELKLINKS.COM

LESSON:

GOD IS TRUTH, HE CANNOT LIE. HIS WORD IS TRUTH. HIS STORY IS BETTER THAN FAIRY TALES.

SCRIPTURE:

SANCTIFY THEM THROUGH THY TRUTH: THY WORD IS TRUTH. JOHN 17:17

FOR THE WORD OF THE LORD IS RIGHT; AND ALL HIS WORKS ARE DONE IN TRUTH. PSALM 33:4

FOR THIS CAUSE ALSO THANK WE GOD WITHOUT CEASING, BECAUSE, WHEN YE RECEIVED THE WORD OF GOD WHICH YE HEARD OF US, YE RECEIVED IT NOT AS THE WORD OF MEN, BUT AS IT IS IN TRUTH, THE WORD OF GOD, WHICH EFFECTUALLY WORKETH ALSO IN YOU THAT BELIEVE. I THESSALONIANS 2:13

Hi Friends!

I know you've heard stories of fairies and monsters and magic before. Sometimes it's hard to know what to believe, and what not to believe isn't it. God's word is not like those fairy tales. God is truth, and he cannot lie. Every word of his Word speaks the truth. God's story also has a happy ending and his story is SO much better than fairy tales.

(continued on the next page)

I want you to read the Christmas story today, from the Bible, if you have one. It's found in Matthew, and Luke, but probably Luke chapter 2 is the best one to read. Think about what it would be like to be Mary, or Joseph, or the Innkeeper, or the Shepherds. What would you have done if you were them? Would you have acted differently? What did Jesus' birth mean for the world and for you especially? Talk about it after you read the story together, and then spend some time in prayer together, thanking God that his story is truth, and his salvation is available to everyone who asks and believes.

Your Truthful Friend, Melk

Mail from Melk

by Katie Hornor
Artwork by Kat Reader

© *Copyright* 2015, Katie Hornor

JANUARY

Cleanse
v. To make someone or something clean

MELK:

IS FOUND WITH A CUP OF CLEAR WATER AND A CUP OF DIRTY/COLORED (FOOD COLORING ADDED) WATER

ACTIVITY:

CLEANSING THE WATER ACTIVITY: ADD DROPS OF CLOROX TO FOOD COLORED WATER UNTIL IT CLEARS (GET VISUAL INSTRUCTIONS AT HTTP://PARADISEPRAISES.COM/MAILFROMMELK)

MATERIALS:

GLASSES, WATER, FOOD COLORING, CLOROX

LESSON:

GOD CLEANSES US FROM OUR SIN

SCRIPTURE:

BUT IF WE WALK IN THE LIGHT, AS HE IS IN THE LIGHT, WE HAVE FELLOWSHIP ONE WITH ANOTHER, AND THE BLOOD OF JESUS CHRIST HIS SON CLEANSETH US FROM ALL SIN. IF WE SAY THAT WE HAVE NO SIN, WE DECEIVE OURSELVES, AND THE TRUTH IS NOT IN US. IF WE CONFESS OUR SINS, HE IS FAITHFUL AND JUST TO FORGIVE US OUR SINS, AND TO CLEANSE US FROM ALL UNRIGHTEOUSNESS. 1 JOHN 1:7-9

Hi there Friend!

Can you believe it's January already! Seems like just last week we were doing Christmas activities together.

Today's lesson is about the cleansing power of God. Did you know that our sins need to be cleansed? It's like when you get your shirt dirty, your mom needs to clean the spot off your shirt. When cleaned it looks fresh and new again.

1 John 1:8 says that "the blood of Jesus Christ [God's] son cleanses us form all sin." When God cleans us he sees us fresh and clean again, just as if we had not sinned.

I have a neat activity for you to do so you can see more of what I mean. Ask you mom or dad to help you, and watch as the water is made clean.

Your Friend, Melk

1

Mail from Melk

Hi there Friend!

Can you believe it's January already! Seems like just last week we were doing Christmas activities together.

Today's lesson is about the cleansing power of God. Did you know that our sins need to be cleansed? It's like when you get your shirt dirty, your mom needs to clean the spot off your shirt. When cleaned it looks fresh and new again.

1 John 1:8 says that "the blood of Jesus Christ [God's] son cleanses us form all sin." When we ask God to forgive our sins, God cleans us. He makes us look fresh and clean again, just as if we had not sinned.

I have a neat activity for you to do to help you understand what I mean. Ask you mom or dad to help you, and watch as the water is made clean.

Have a great day!
I'll see you again next month!
Your Friend, Melk

January

FEBRUARY

MELK:

IS FOUND WITH WITH A PAD OR PILE OF FUN WRITING PAPERS AND ENVELOPED, HEARTS, STICKERS, (WHATEVER YOU'D LIKE TO USE).

ACTIVITY:

WRITING A LETTER OF LOVE OR APPRECIATION TO SOMEONE (FIND DOWNLOADS & MORE FUND STUFF AT HTTP://PARADISEPRAISES.COM/MAILFROMMELK)

MATERIALS:

PAPER, PENS, PENCILS (OPTIONAL: MARKERS, ENVELOPES, STICKERS, FOAM CUTOUT HEARTS, GLITTER, CONFETTI, ETC.)

LESSON:

GOD DECLARES HIS LOVE FOR US

SCRIPTURE:

FOR GOD SO LOVED THE WORLD THAT HE GAVE HIS ONLY BEGOTTEN SON, THAT WHOSOEVER BELIEVETH IN HIM SHOULD NOT PERISH, BUT HAVE EVERLASTING LIFE. JOHN 3:16

FOR GREAT IS HIS STEADFAST LOVE TOWARD US, AND THE FAITHFULNESS OF THE LORD ENDURES FOREVER. PRAISE THE LORD! PSALM 117:2

BELOVED, LET US LOVE ONE ANOTHER, FOR LOVE IS FROM GOD, AND WHOEVER LOVES HAS BEEN BORN OF GOD AND KNOWS GOD. 1 JOHN 4:7

Love
n. strong affection for another arising out of kinship or personal ties

n. unselfish loyal and benevolent concern for the good of another

Hi there Friend!

Happy February! This is the shortest month of the year, and also the month in which lots of people do something special for the people they love. Do you know who loves you more than anyone else in the whole, wide world?

That's right! God loves you more than anyone else. And what's more, Romans 8:35-39 says that NOTHING can separate us from God's love. No matter what you do or don't do he loves you just the same. His love is based on who he is, not on what you do.

How does God tell us about his love? You're right again! He tells us in the Bible. It's like he has written a great big love letter to us telling us all about who he is and how he loves us.

Don't you love to get letters and email? Today I want you to write a letter to someone you love and tell them why and how much you love them, and you might tell them how much God loves them too! If you're not quite big enough to write, you can tell your Mom or Dad what to write and they'll help you.

Never forget that God loves you more than anyone who ever lived! You are special to him.
Your Loving Friend, Melk

Mail from Melk

Hi there Friend!

Happy February! This is the shortest month of the year, and also the month in which lots of people do something special for the people they love. Do you know who loves you more than anyone else in the whole, wide world?

That's right! God loves you more than anyone else. And what's more, Romans 8:35-39 says that NOTHING can separate us from God's love. No matter what you do or don't do he loves you just the same. His love is based on who he is, not on what you do.

How does God tell us about his love? You're right again! He tells us in the Bible. It's like he has written a great big love letter to us telling us all about who he is and how he loves us.

Don't you love to get letters and email? Today I want you to write a letter to someone you love and tell them why and how much you love them, and you might tell them how much God loves them too! If you're not quite big enough to write, you can tell your Mom or Dad what to write and they'll help you.

Never forget that God loves you more than anyone who ever lived! You are special to him.

Your Loving Friend, Melk

February

MARCH

MELK:

IS FOUND IN A PILE OF 3-LEAFED CLOVERS (PAPER CUT OUTS, FOAM SHAPES, CONFETTI, REAL ONES, WHATEVER YOU'D LIKE TO USE). AND THE DOWNLOADED ACTIVITY SHEET AND SOMETHING TO WRITE WITH.

ACTIVITY:

UNDERSTANDING THE TRIUNE CHARACTERISTIC OF GOD.

(NOTE: THIS IS NOT A CELEBRATION OF ST. PATRICK, THOUGH HE IS CREDITED WITH FIRST USING THIS ILLUSTRATION. YOU MAY MENTION HIM OR NOT AS YOU CHOOSE. IF YOU WOULD LIKE TO SEE ST. PATRICK'S DAY CRAFTS, IDEAS AND ACTIVITIES, PLEASE VISIT OUR ST. PATRICK'S DAY PINTEREST BOARD. HTTPS://WWW.PINTEREST.COM/PARADISEPRAISES/HOLIDAYST-PATRICKS-DAY/)

MATERIALS:

PRINTED ACTIVITY SHEET, PEN, PENCIL, 3-LEAFED CLOVERS

LESSON:

GOD IS 3 DISTINCT PEOPLE, BUT ALL ONE GOD.

SCRIPTURE:

FOR THERE ARE THREE THAT BEAR RECORD IN HEAVEN, THE FATHER, THE WORD, AND THE HOLY GHOST: AND THESE THREE ARE ONE. 1 JOHN 5:7

Triune

a. of or relating to the Trinity, the (the triune God)

a. consisting of three parts, members, or aspects

Hi there Friend!

Can you believe it is March already! By the end of this month 1/4 of this year will be over already! It's going by quickly, and before you know it Christmas will be here again!

Speaking of numbers, did you know that God is 3 people all in one? He is! He is God, the Father, God the Son, and God the Holy Spirit. God the Father created the world. God the Son (Jesus) died for us on the cross, so we could be forgiven of our sins and accepted into God's presence again. And God the Holy Spirit never leaves us once we are forgiven and adopted by God. And yet, he is all the same person! Pretty amazing isn't it!

To help you understand, I want you to look at these clovers. Do you see the 3 leaves? It is one clover, but it has 3 leaves, right? Leaf #1. Leaf #2. And Leaf #3. It's not 3 clovers, it is 1 clover with 3 leaves. God is one God in 3 persons.

I want you to think of other things that are 3 in one. You can talk about them with your family and write them on this paper.

Remember God is always with you! I'll see you next month!
Your Amazed by God's greatness Friend,
Melk

Mail from Melk

Hi there Friend!

Can you believe it is March already! By the end of this month 1/4 of this year will be over already! It's going by quickly, and before you know it Christmas will be here again!

Speaking of numbers, did you know that God is 3 people all in one? He is! He is God, the Father, God the Son, and God the Holy Spirit. God the Father created the world. God the Son (Jesus) died for us on the cross, so we could be forgiven of our sins and accepted into God's presence again. And God the Holy Spirit never leaves us once we are forgiven and adopted by God. And yet, he is all the same person! Pretty amazing isn't it!

To help you understand, I want you to look at these clovers. Do you see the 3 leaves? It is one clover, but it has 3 leaves, right? Leaf #1. Leaf #2. And Leaf #3. It's not 3 clovers, it is 1 clover with 3 leaves. God is one God in 3 persons.

I want you to think of other things that are 3 in one. You can talk about them with your family and write them on this paper.

Remember God is always with you! I'll see you next month!
Your Amazed by God's greatness Friend,
Melk

March

APRIL

King
n. ruler, sovereign, monarch, crowned head of state.

MELK:

IS FOUND WEARING A KING'S CROWN.

ACTIVITY:

MAKING A PAPER CROWN

MATERIALS:

PRE-CUT CROWNS FROM YOUR LOCAL CRAFT STORE OR PAPER, SCISSORS, MARKERS, GLUE GLITTER, STICKERS ETC. (LINKS TO CROWNS AND PRINTABLE PATTERNS AT HTTP://PARADISEPRAISES.COM/MAIL-MELK/)

LESSON:

GOD IS THE KING OF KINGS, RULER OF ALL.

SCRIPTURE:

WHICH IN HIS TIMES HE SHALL SHEW, WHO IS THE BLESSED AND ONLY POTENTATE, THE KING OF KINGS, AND LORD OF LORDS. 1 TIMOTHY 6:15

THESE SHALL MAKE WAR WITH THE LAMB, AND THE LAMB SHALL OVERCOME THEM: FOR HE IS LORD OF LORDS, AND KING OF KINGS: AND THEY THAT ARE WITH HIM ARE CALLED, AND CHOSEN, AND FAITHFUL. REVELATION 17:14

AND HE HATH ON HIS VESTURE AND ON HIS THIGH A NAME WRITTEN, KING OF KINGS, AND LORD OF LORDS. REVELATION 19:16

Hi there Friend!

Do you see my crown? Today we're going to make one for you too to remind us that God is our King, the King of Kings!

A King is a ruler. The top person in charge. The people under his rule obey him and also look to him for protection and leadership. All throughout history, there have been good kings and bad kings. The bad kings were usually selfish and mean to others and only looking out for themselves.

God is always good and honest and just. He is the best King of all Kings. He loves us, and always wants what is best for us. He provides for our needs and shows us (through his Words in the Bible) what we should and should not do to please him and love others.

When we accept God's forgiveness from our sins and His free gift of salvation, he makes us an heir to his throne! He makes us his child, and one day when our physical body dies, we will go to heaven to live in a mansion in the presence of the King of Kings!

That's pretty awesome isn't it! Every time you see a crown, I want you to remember that God is the King of Kings and that you can live with him for ever!

Your Friend,

Melk

1

Hi there Friend!

Do you see my crown? Today we're going to make one for you too to remind us that God is our King, the King of Kings!

A King is a ruler. The top person in charge. The people under his rule obey him and also look to him for protection and leadership. All throughout history, there have been good kings and bad kings. The bad kings were usually selfish and mean to others and only looking out for themselves.

God is always good and honest and just. He is the best King of all Kings. He loves us, and always wants what is best for us. He provides for our needs and shows us (through his Words in the Bible) what we should and should not do to please him and love others.

When we accept God's forgiveness from our sins and His free gift of salvation, he makes us an heir to his throne! He makes us his child, and one day when our physical body dies, we will go to heaven to live in a mansion in the pressence of the King of Kings!

That's pretty awesome isn't it! Every time you see a crown, I want you to remember that God is the King of Kings and that you can live with him for ever!

Your Friend,
Melk

April

MAY

MELK:

IS FOUND READING A BIBLE.

ACTIVITY:

MAKE YOUR OWN SWORD AND SHIELD

MATERIALS:

CARDBOARD, PAPER, SCISSORS, MARKERS, DUCT TAPE, GLUE, GLITTER, STICKERS ETC. (LINKS TO PRINTABLE PATTERNS AND INSTRUCTIONS AT HTTP://PARADISEPRAISES.COM/MAIL-MELK/)

LESSON:

GOD IS OUR PROTECTOR.

SCRIPTURE:

HE SHALL COVER THEE WITH HIS FEATHERS, AND UNDER HIS WINGS SHALT THOU TRUST: HIS TRUTH SHALL BE THY SHIELD AND BUCKLER. PSALM 91:4

FOR THE LORD GOD IS A SUN AND SHIELD: THE LORD WILL GIVE GRACE AND GLORY: NO GOOD THING WILL HE WITHHOLD FROM THEM THAT WALK UPRIGHTLY. PSALM 84:11

THE GOD OF MY ROCK; IN HIM WILL I TRUST: HE IS MY SHIELD, AND THE HORN OF MY SALVATION, MY HIGH TOWER, AND MY REFUGE, MY SAVIOUR; THOU SAVEST ME FROM VIOLENCE. 2 SAMUEL 22:3

GOD IS OUR PROTECTOR

Protector
n. a person or thing that protects someone or something.

historical meaning: a person in charge of a kingdom during the minority, absence, or incapacity of the sovereign.

Hi there Friend!

I was just reading about God being our protector! The Bible says he is a shield for us, and that we can trust him.

Just like the kings of old would go into battle with their men to protect their people and lands, the Lord fights for us. He protects us. What's even more great about it is that God is more powerful than anything and anyone! Nothing can ever harm us without God knowing, and if he doesn't want it to happen, he is powerful enough to stop it.

Today, we're going to make a shield of our own and everytime we play with it or see it, we will remember that God is our shiled. He is our great protector!

Your Protected Friend,
Melk

Hi there Friend!

I was just reading about God being our protector! The Bible says he is a shield for us, and that we can trust him.

Just like the kings of old would go into battle with their men to protect their people and lands, the Lord fights for us. He protects us. What's even more great about it is that God is more powerful than anything and anyone! Nothing can ever harm us without God knowing, and if he doesn't want it to happen, he is powerful enough to stop it.

Today, we're going to make a shield of our own and everytime we play with it or see it, we will remember that God is our shiled. He is our great protector!

Your Protected Friend,
Melk

May

JUNE

MELK:

MELK IS FOUND IN A TENT (UNDER A BOOK?) WITH A PRETEND CAMPFIRE (IF YOU HAVE NO SMALL TWIGS AVAILABLE TRY USING CRAYONS TO SUGGEST A CAMPFIRE)

protect
v. To keep safe from harm, watch over, look after

ACTIVITY:

CAMPOUT IN YOUR BACKYARD, OR YOUR LIVING ROOM OR MAKE A TENT FOR YOUR MELK AND LET HIM CAMP OUT (GET TOY TENT INSTRUCTIONS AT HTTP://PARADISEPRAISES.COM/MAIL-MELK)

MATERIALS:

BOOK, CRAYONS, TWIGS, FABRIC, STICKS, PRE-MADE TENT, CAMPING GEAR

LESSON:

GOD NEVER SLEEPS AND HE ALONE CAN KEEP US SAFE.

SCRIPTURE:

HE THAT KEEPETH THEE WILL NOT SLUMBER. PSALM 121:3B

I WILL BOTH LAY ME DOWN IN PEACE, AND SLEEP: FOR THOU, LORD, ONLY MAKEST ME DWELL IN SAFETY. PSALM 4:8

Hi there Friend!

Have you ever gone camping? or slept in a new place for the first time? Was is scary? Were there things you weren't used to seeing in the dark? or sounds you weren't used to hearing? Was it hard to go to sleep?

Did you know that God never sleeps? He is always awake. That is how he can hear our prayers anytime of day or night, no matter where we are. That is also how he always protects us. We don't need to be afraid when we know that God is with us.

Psalm 4:8 says "I will both lay me down in peace, and sleep: for Thou, Lord, Only makest me dwell in safety." When you are camping or you are somewhere else and you are afraid of the dark, I want you to remember that God is with you and he can hear you when you pray to him. You can sleep in peace because He is with you and He loves you more than anyone else in the whole world.

Until next time,
Your Friend, Melk

Mail from Melk

Hi there Friend!

Have you ever gone camping? or slept in a new place for the first time? Was is scary? Were there things you weren't used to seeing in the dark? or sounds you weren't used to hearing? Was it hard to go to sleep?

Did you know that God never sleeps? He is always awake. That is how he can hear our prayers anytime of day or night, no matter where we are. That is also how he always protects us. We don't need to be afraid when we know that God is with us.

Psalm 4:8 says "I will both lay me down in peace, and sleep: for Thou, Lord, Only makest me dwell in safety." When you are camping or you are somewhere else and you are afraid of the dark, I want you to remember that God is with you and he can hear you when you pray to him. You can sleep in peace because He is with you and He loves you more than anyone else in the whole world.

Until next time,
Your Friend, Melk

June

JULY

MELK:

MELK IS FOUND WITH A BASKET OR BOX OF FUN SURPRISES TO TAKE TO A FRIEND OR A FAMILY IN NEED.

ACTIVITY:

CREATE CARDS, WRITE LETTERS, BAKE GOODIES AND/OR PURCHASE SMALL SURPRISES TO GIFT TO A FRIEND OR A FAMILY IN NEED AS A JUST-BECAUSE SURPRISE.

MATERIALS:

PAPER, ART SUPPLIES, SMALL BAG OR BASKET, GIFTS (OPTIONAL) FOR IDEAS, PRINTABLES AND RECIPES CHECK OUT OUR "SUNSHINE BOX" BOARD ON PINTEREST: HTTPS://WWW.PINTEREST.COM/PARADISEPRAISES/SUNSHINE-BOXES/

LESSON:

GOD GIVES GOOD GIFTS

SCRIPTURE:

EVERY GOOD GIFT AND EVERY PERFECT GIFT IS FROM ABOVE, AND COMETH DOWN FROM THE FATHER OF LIGHTS, WITH WHOM IS NO VARIABLENESS, NEITHER SHADOW OF TURNING. JAMES 1:17

I HAVE SHEWED YOU ALL THINGS, HOW THAT SO LABOURING YE OUGHT TO SUPPORT THE WEAK, AND TO REMEMBER THE WORDS OF THE LORD JESUS, HOW HE SAID, IT IS MORE BLESSED TO GIVE THAN TO RECEIVE. ACTS

give

v. 1. freely transfer the possession of (something) to (someone); hand over to.

2. cause or allow (someone or something) to have (something, especially something abstract); provide or supply with.

Hi there Friend!

Have you ever thought about all of the good things God gives you and I? We don't deserve them, do we? But he gives them anyway because HE is good and He loves us.

His Word tells us that Every good gift and every perfect gift is from above, and cometh down from the Father of lights, with whom is no variableness, neither shadow of turning. (James 1:17) and it also tells us that it is more blessed (or happy) to give than to receive (Acts 20:35).

Our special activity for today is to create a surprise gift for a friend or a family that you know that is having a hard time, or needs to be cheered up. They need to be reminded of God's love and of his good gifts for them. We're going to create some cards for them and take them a special gift. And doing so will bless us and make us happy as well! I can't wait to hear how it goes! Will you write me a letter and let me know?

Smiley and Happy,
Your Friend, Melk

1

Mail from Melk

Hi there Friend!

Have you ever thought about all of the good things God gives you and I? We don't deserve them, do we? But he gives them anyway because HE is good and He loves us.

His Word tells us that Every good gift and every perfect gift is from above, and cometh down from the Father of lights, with whom is no variableness, neither shadow of turning. (James 1:17) and it also tells us that it is more blessed (or happy) to give than to receive (Acts 20:35).

Our special activity for today is to create a surprise gift for a friend or a family that you know that is having a hard time, or needs to be cheered up. They need to be reminded of God's love and of his good gifts for them. We're going to create some cards for them and take them a special gift. And doing so will bless us and make us happy as well! I can't wait to hear how it goes! Will you write me a letter and let me know?

Smiley and Happy,
Your Friend, Melk

July

AUGUST

eternal
adj. lasting or existing forever; without end or beginning. Valid for all time; essentially unchanging.

MELK:

MELK IS FOUND WITH AN EMPTY PLASTIC DRINK BOTTLE

ACTIVITY:

CREATE A WATER FOUNTAIN TO PLAY WITH OUTDOORS

MATERIALS:

CLEAN EMPTY POP BOTTLE, NAIL (OR POINTED OBJECT TO POKE HOLES IN THE BOTTLE), DUCT TAPE, WATER HOSE AND THESE INSTRUCTIONS FROM PINTEREST: HTTPS://WWW.PINTEREST.COM/PIN/291748882088224623/

NOTE: IF YOU DON'T HAVE THE WATER PRESSURE TO MAKE IT SPRAY YOU CAN DO YOUR HOLES IN THE BOTTOM OF THE BOTTLE AND HANG YOUR FOUNTAIN SO THE WATER POURS DOWN FROM ABOVE.

LESSON:

GOD GIVES ETERNAL LIFE THAT SPRINGS UP WITHIN US LIKE A FOUNTAIN

SCRIPTURE:

BUT WHOSOEVER DRINKETH OF THE WATER THAT I SHALL GIVE HIM SHALL NEVER THIRST; BUT THE WATER THAT I SHALL GIVE HIM SHALL BE IN HIM A WELL OF WATER SPRINGING UP INTO EVERLASTING LIFE. JOHN 4:14

DROP DOWN, YE HEAVENS, FROM ABOVE, AND LET THE SKIES POUR DOWN RIGHTEOUSNESS: LET THE EARTH OPEN, AND LET THEM BRING FORTH SALVATION, AND LET RIGHTEOUSNESS SPRING UP TOGETHER; I THE LORD HAVE CREATED IT. ISAIAH 45:8

Hi there Friend!

Have you ever seen a water fountain? I mean a really big one? Isn't it fun to watch and play in? All who get near it get wet with the spray.

God's Word tells us that salvation is like a well of water springing up within us. It should be very obvious to all who get close to us that we belong to the Lord and have his gift of eternal life springing up inside of us.

Would you like to create a fountain today? Ask your parent or another adult to help you create the garden hose water fountain that I sent them instructions for. Then enjoy playing in your fountain and give thanks to the One who gives us the Living Water of Eternal Life.

Your Friend, Melk
P.S.
All of our activity links can be found here: http://paradisepraises.com/mail-melk/

Mail from Melk

Hi there Friend!

Have you ever seen a water fountain? I mean a really big one? Isn't it fun to watch and play in? All who get near it get wet with the spray.

God's Word tells us that salvation is like a well of water springing up within us. It should be very obvious to all who get close to us that we belong to the Lord and have his gift of eternal life springing up inside of us.

Would you like to create a fountain today? Ask your parent or another adult to help you create the garden hose water fountain that I sent them instructions for. Then enjoy playing in your fountain and give thanks to the One who gives us the Living Water of Eternal Life.
Your Friend, Melk

August

SEPTEMBER

give

v. to grant relief from payment of

MELK:

MELK IS FOUND WITH PAPERS (OR FELT) OF SEVERAL COLORS

ACTIVITY:

MAKE A WORDLESS BOOK

MATERIALS:

PAPER BOOK: PAPERS OF DIFFERENT COLORS, GLUE, STAPLER, SCISSORS

FELT BOOK: FELT OF DIFFERENT COLORS, SCISSORS, NEEDLE AND THREAD

FIND INSTRUCTIONS FOR MAKING A WORDLESS BOOK HERE: HTTP://PARADISEPRAISES.COM/MAIL-MELK

LESSON:

GOD FORGIVES OUR SIN, DOES NOT REQUIRE THAT WE PAY THE PENALTY ANY LONGER BECAUSE CHRIST PAYED IT FOR US.

SCRIPTURE:

FOR THE WAGES OF SIN IS DEATH, BUT THE GIFT OF GOD IS ETERNAL LIFE THROUGH JESUS CHRIST, OUR LORD. ROMANS 6:23

IF WE CONFESS OUR SINS, HE IS FAITHFUL AND JUST TO FORGIVE US OUR SINS, AND TO CLEANSE US FROM ALL UNRIGHTEOUSNESS. 1 JOHN 1:9

Hi there Friend!

I was just sitting here looking at these beautiful colors and it reminded me of something... a story of life.

Did you know that our lives are dark like this color black, because of our sins. And that the price or payment God requires for sin is death? We cannot be good without God's help and we need his forgiveness from our sin and the cost of it.

The red color reminds me of good news though. That good news is that when Jesus died on the cross, he died to pay the price of those sins, so that through him, we can be forgiven by God. Isn't that amazing!

Ask your mom or dad to help you make a wordless book today, to learn the meanings of the colors and how to tell the story to others using your book without words.

Happy to be forgiven,
Your Friend, Melk

Mail from Melk

Hi there Friend!

I was just sitting here looking at these beautiful colors and it reminded me of something... a story of life.

Did you know that our lives are dark like this color black, because of our sins. And that the price or payment God requires for sin is death? We cannot be good without God's help and we need his forgiveness from our sin and the cost of it.

The red color reminds me of good news though. That good news is that when Jesus died on the cross, he died to pay the price of those sins, so that through him, we can be forgiven by God. Isn't that amazing!

Ask your mom or dad to help you make a wordless book today, to learn the meanings of the colors and how to tell the story to others using your book without words.

Happy to be forgiven,

September

OCTOBER

Omnipresent
Adj. presentverywhere all at the same time

MELK:

MELK IS FOUND WITH A PAPER PASSPORT

ACTIVITY:

MAKE A PAPER PASSPORT AND STAMPS

MATERIALS:

PRINTOUTS, SCISSORS, GLUE, CRAYONS/PENCILS

FIND INSTRUCTIONS AND PRINTABLES FOR THE PRINTABLE PASSPORT KIT HERE: HTTP://PARADISEPRAISES.COM/MAIL-MELK

LESSON:

GOD IS EVERYWHERE ALL AT ONE TIME, AND HEARS AND CARES FOR US ALL AT ONCE. HE IS WITH ME ALWAYS, NO MATTER WHERE I AM.

SCRIPTURE:

WHITHER SHALL I GO FROM THY SPIRIT? OR WHITHER SHALL I FLEE FROM THY PRESENCE? IF I ASCEND UP INTO HEAVEN, THOU ART THERE: IF I MAKE MY BED IN HELL, BEHOLD, THOU ART THERE. IF I TAKE THE WINGS OF THE MORNING, AND DWELL IN THE UTTERMOST PARTS OF THE SEA; EVEN THERE SHALL THY HAND LEAD ME, AND THY RIGHT HAND SHALL HOLD ME. PSALM 139:7-10

Hi there Friend!

I have my passport with me today. Do you have a passport? Have you ever visited a different country? It is different there isn't it? They may dress different, and eat differnt foods than we do. They may even get up and go to bed at different times.

But even for all of their differences, God loves them and is with them all of the time, just as he loves us and is with us all of the time.

The Bible says that we cannot go anywhere that God is not. He is everywhere all at the same time and ready to lead us and protect us and love us (Psalm 139:7-10).

Today, I brought you a passport kit so you can make your own passport and pretend to visit other countries. As you do, don't forget to get your passport stamped! And dont' forget that you can never go anywhere where God is not. He is always with you!

Your traveling Friend,
    Melk

Mail from Melk

Hi there Friend!

I have my passport with me today. Do you have a passport? Have you ever visited a different country? It is different there isn't it? They may dress different, and eat differnt foods than we do. They may even get up and go to bed at different times.

But even for all of their differences, God loves them and is with them all of the time, just as he loves us and is with us all of the time.

The Bible says that we cannot go anywhere that God is not. He is everywhere all at the same time and ready to lead us and protect us and love us (Psalm 139:7-10)

Today, I brought you a passport kit so you can make your own passport and pretend to visit other countries. As you do, don't forget to get your passport stamped! And dont' forget that you can never go anywhere where God is not. He is always with you!

Your traveling Friend,

October

NOVEMBER

Gracious
Adj. characterized by charm, good taste, generosity of spirit, and the tasteful leisure of wealth and good breeding.

MELK:

MELK IS FOUND WITH A THE CARDS, DICE AND INSTRUCTIONS FOR THE THANKFUL GAME.

ACTIVITY:

PLAY THE THANKFUL GAME TOGETHER, AS A FAMILY.

MATERIALS:

PRINTOUTS, SCISSORS, DICE

FIND INSTRUCTIONS AND PRINTABLES FOR THE THANKFUL GAME HERE: HTTP://PARADISEPRAISES.COM/MAIL-MELK

LESSON:

GOD IS A GRACIOUS, GIVING GOD, AND DESERVES OUR THANKS.

SCRIPTURE:

BUT THOU, O LORD, ART A GOD FULL OF COMPASSION, AND GRACIOUS, LONG SUFFERING, AND PLENTEOUS IN MERCY AND TRUTH. PSALM 86:15

O GIVE THANKS UNTO THE LORD; CALL UPON HIS NAME: MAKE KNOWN HIS DEEDS AMONG THE PEOPLE. PSALM 105:1

IT IS A GOOD THING TO GIVE THANKS UNTO THE LORD, AND TO SING PRAISES UNTO THY NAME, O MOST HIGH: PSALM 92:1

Well, hello again!

Today I have a question for you... well 2 questions... When was the last time you thanked God for something? And Did you know it is hard to be grateful and in a bad mood at the same time?

In November, in the USA, the fourth Thursday is a holiday specifically set aside as a day to be thankful. Whether you are in the USA or in another country, it is still a great idea to show your thanks to the Lord for the things he has done for you and given to you, and I have something to help you do that!

God give us so many good gifts! You can use the Thankful Game cards and this dice to take turns with your family expressing your thanks to the Lord. Don't worry, I've given you some clues for what to say. Have fun!

Your thankful Friend,
    Melk

Mail from Melk

Well, hello again!

Today I have a question for you... well 2 questions... When was the last time you thanked God for something? And Did you know it is hard to be grateful and in a bad mood at the same time?

In November, in the USA, the fourth Thursday is a holiday specifically set aside as a day to be thankful. Whether you are in the USA or in another country, it is still a great idea to show your thanks to the Lord for the things he has done for you and given to you, and I have something to help you do that!

God give us so many good gifts! You can use the Thankful Game cards and this dice to take turns with your family expressing your thanks to the Lord. Don't worry, I've given you some clues for what to say. Have fun!

Your thankful Friend,
        Melk

                                                        November

Made in the USA
Monee, IL
22 March 2024